LOVE TAKING SHAPE

LOVE TAKING SHAPE

Sermons on the Christian Life

GILBERT MEILAENDER

William B. Eerdmans Publishing Company

Grand Rapids, Michigan / Cambridge, U.K.

© 2002 Wm. B. Eerdmans Publishing Co.
All rights reserved

Wm. B. Eerdmans Publishing Co.
255 Jefferson Ave. S.E., Grand Rapids, Michigan 49503 /
P.O. Box 163, Cambridge CB3 9PU U.K.

Printed in the United States of America

06 05 04 03 02   5 4 3 2 1

Library of Congress Cataloging-in-Publication Data

Meilaender, Gilbert, 1946-
Love taking shape : sermons on the Christian life / Gilbert Meilaender.
p.   cm.
ISBN 0-8028-3952-5 (pbk. : alk. paper)
1. Christian life — Sermons.   I. Title.
BV4501.3 .M45   2002

252'.041 — dc21

2001058455

www.eerdmans.com

To the saints at

Grace Lutheran Church, Oberlin, Ohio

Grace Lutheran Church, Elyria, Ohio

SS. Peter & Paul Lutheran Church, Lorain, Ohio

St. Paul Lutheran Church, Amherst, Ohio

Shepherd of the Ridge Lutheran Church, N. Ridgeville, Ohio

Contents

Contents

Preface

The sermons about the Christian life collected here are written by an academician — indeed, one who teaches ethics — but they are, nevertheless, sermons. They have been preached (to Lutheran congregations), and, since my preaching is not confined to a single congregation, many of them have been preached more than once. But this is not intended to be a book from which other preachers might draw their sermons. Not much believing in that form of sermon preparation, I would not offer these for such use. Rather, they are my attempt to preach about what I also teach. Some things should be preached and others taught, though, so the two tasks are not the same. I have little doubt that, of the two, preaching is the more difficult. These sermons are offered, then, as one kind of reflection — in what we may even call a particular genre — about how love takes shape in the Christian life.

If the sermon is a mode of communication in which we must address not a select few but an entire body of believers, it is also — we may be glad — a genre in which we are permitted to borrow liberally from all whom we have read and by whom we have been influenced. In the short introduction to each section of sermons I have tried to note, where I can recall, the thinkers whose influence is apparent in those sermons. Some, though not all, of the sermons were preached on lessons appointed for a particular Sunday in the liturgical year. But, contrary to what I was taught in seminary, a sermon must grow out of the whole of one's theological study and reflection, not just out of the encounter with a particular text. I thankfully acknowledge, therefore, my dependence on all from whom I have learned to think theologically.

Many years ago in seminary I took a class in practical theology taught by Professor George Hoyer. I remember absolutely nothing from that class except one sentence. In the course of a discussion, in which somehow the topic of clergy impatience with parishioners had arisen, Professor Hoyer said: "Just remember that these people are coming back to hear you Sunday after Sunday — and you're not always so good." I therefore acknowledge my gratitude to all those who, because they came to hear these sermons, forced upon me the struggle and reflection they represent.

Finally, I would not have a reader of this volume think that I am ignorant of the rules of punctuation or unable to write complete sentences. But a sermon is meant to be preached, and preaching has its own cadence, not bound by our normal rules of punctuation. I have, therefore, felt free to write as if speaking and as if these pages were to be read aloud.

I. Buried with Christ: Homilies for Lent

Among American Lutherans it has been quite common practice to have special services on the Wednesday evenings of Lent. I do not think these services cut as deeply into people's lives as they did when I was young, but the practice continues. Years ago the preaching in these services tended to focus on the cross — characters of the passion narrative, Jesus' words on the cross, hymns of the passion, and so forth. Those dominated Lenten preaching until liturgical renewal movements began to frown on such simplicity and to suggest that this never-ending march around the cross was not what Lent should involve. If Lent was originally a time when catechumens were prepared for baptism at Easter, its focus, we were told, should be on Christian living. I have occasionally found myself wondering whether this shift does not partially account for the fact that Lenten services no longer cut as deeply into the lives of parishioners. When Lent becomes principally a time for us to occupy ourselves with works of repentance, reconciliation, and love in preparation for a renewal of our baptism at Easter, we too easily image the Christian life as movement toward, rather than from, baptism — movement toward, rather than from, forgiveness.

In any case, someone should have noted how peculiar it was that, at exactly the time when theology was recapturing the significance of "narrative," Lenten preaching should have been indicted for taking six weeks to contemplate the story of Jesus' passion — which is, after all, the one connected narrative the Gospels present. There may be times when it is best just to tell and retell the story.

Nevertheless, the five short homilies that follow are an attempt to capture a little of both emphases. Originally preached in services of Evening Prayer on the five Wednesdays following Ash Wednesday, they attempt to preach a coherent set of homilies which are both catechetical in nature and connected to Jesus' passion. All five have their root in Romans 6; all five make use of the questions and answers about baptism in Luther's *Small Catechism*.

My treatment of baptism's significance, especially with respect to the nature of "promise," has been considerably influenced by Robert Jenson's *Visible Words*. The distinction between grace as pardon and as power in the fourth and fifth homilies, though in many ways standard Christian fare, is drawn rather directly from the second volume of Reinhold Niebuhr's *The Nature and Destiny of Man*. Beyond that, I have attempted simply to think through the meaning of Romans 6 and have not attempted to hide my conviction that Luther's four brief questions and answers about baptism contain almost everything one needs to say.

1. *Water*

*Do you not know that all of us who have been baptized
into Christ Jesus were baptized into his death? We were
buried therefore with him by baptism into death, so that
as Christ was raised from the dead by the glory of the Father, we too might walk in newness of life.*

ROMANS 6:3-4

Why baptism? Why talk about baptism during these weeks of
Lent? We may tend to think of Lent as that season of the
church year when we remember especially the passion of Jesus, and we may be inclined to ask, what has baptism to do
with that?

We should be careful about asking such a question,
though, when we have just heard St. Paul say that being baptized into Christ is being baptized into his death. Maybe the
connection between Lent and baptism is deeper than we
know or think. Indeed, if we go far enough back in the
church's history, we discover that the time of Lent developed

not primarily as a time to focus upon Jesus' passion but as a time in which catechumens completed their instruction and prepared to renounce the world and be baptized into the faith at Easter. Lent has from the very start been connected with baptism, and it is a time for teaching and re-teaching the essentials of the faith.

The connection of baptism and Lent is also something deeper than this historical tie, however, and to see this will be to see that we are not wrong in Lent to focus our attention upon the cross. There is a theological connection to be forged, an inescapable bond, between baptism and Jesus' passion. To that bond St. Paul points in Romans 6: "Do you not know that all of us who have been baptized into Christ Jesus were baptized into his death?" That was the bond Dietrich Bonhoeffer had in mind when he wrote, "When Christ calls a man, he bids him come and die." By baptism we are made participants in the death of Christ, a death to the powers that dominate our world and our natural life. We can say, then, that we never speak adequately about Christ's passion unless we also eventually speak of our baptism, and we never speak adequately of our baptism unless we connect it to the cross and grave of our Lord.

When we talk of baptism, therefore, we talk of the death to which Christ calls each of us and the promise of new life he offers. *What is Baptism?* Luther asked in his *Small Catechism.* A seemingly simple question to which Luther gives a simple but profound answer. *Baptism is not simple water only, but it is the water comprehended in God's command and connected with God's word.* In its most elemental sense baptism is water and word. A washing with water — commanded by God's word. A washing with water — to which is attached the word of God's promise. For today it will be enough to think about the water — to remind ourselves that baptism is a washing with water.

At least since the time of St. Augustine some 1600 years ago, the sacraments have often been called "visible words." Words in which the hidden God shows himself in our world and speaks to us. Words we can touch and feel and see and taste — not just words for the ear to hear. Visible words. Bread and wine for me to eat. Water to cleanse me.

The spoken word is, of course, important — even crucial. We could not get along without it, and we will explore its significance next week. But the water of baptism is a visible word. It's simply there, poured on us. It confronts us with its givenness. The spoken word I can just not listen to or fail to hear. (Have you never daydreamed your way through a sermon?) I can fail to hear — and therefore miss the fact that the spoken word is directed to me. But pour water on me or dunk me in water and I cannot miss the fact that this action is aimed at me. That I am myself involved. The visible word, the water in baptism, involves us right here in the world of everyday life, the world of objects and bodies. There's a sense, of course, in which anything, any object, any visible word might accomplish that; and yet, water is somehow just right, isn't it? Water — that God parted at the Red Sea in a mighty act of deliverance. Water — without which we cannot live. Water — which, mingled with blood, ran from the crucified Savior's side. Water — that washes us clean.

In that water God meets us and makes us his. In our bodies we touch one another. Indeed, it is not wrong to say that we *are* our bodies. We can talk about the spirit all we like, but when I feel those pains in my chest I run to the doctor. When

I ache all over with a high fever, I get to the doctor. And I don't say, "Doctor, there's something wrong with my body, with this thing I carry around." I say, "Doctor, *I* am sick." We are our bodies, because God has made us from the dust of the ground. And here, in this world of bodies, God meets us and touches us with something we can see and feel and taste — with the water of our baptism.

God washes us with that water, that we may be clean. That in this washing we may be baptized into the death of Christ and buried with him — dead to the powers of sin that dominate our world. Alive with freedom to walk in newness of life. Alive to the hope that for us too Easter will one day come.

2. Word

For if we have been united with him in a death like his, we shall certainly be united with him in a resurrection like his.

ROMANS 6:5

What is baptism? Water comprehended in God's command and connected with God's word. That is Luther's answer in his *Small Catechism*. Baptism is a washing with water — but a washing connected to the command and the promise of God. For when Luther asked himself, *What does baptism give or profit?* he answered: *It works forgiveness of sins, delivers from death and the devil, and gives eternal salvation. . . .* And that, in turn, forced him to ask, *How can water do such great things?* and to answer: *It is not the water indeed that does them, but the word of God which is in and with the water. . . .*

Baptism is water + word. What does the word add to the simple fact of washing with water? The word adds both command and promise. We are commanded to wash with water in the name of the Triune God. We are promised that doing so will make us participants in the death and resurrection of Christ.

Baptism is commanded by Christ. Luther quotes that command: *Christ our Lord says in the last chapter of Matthew: Go ye and teach all nations, baptizing them. . . .* Why do we baptize? Because the crucified and risen Lord of the church tells us to. Not because we think washing with water is a fitting ritual for cleansing and initiation. No doubt it is that, but we do not baptize for that reason. There might, after all, be other good ways to accept people into the church. We could sing a song to the newly initiated one, or give her a round of applause. Nice ideas perhaps, but not the rite of initiation commanded by the word of Christ.

We do what he has commanded us to. You and I have been baptized because the church has been faithful to that command. For in the command Christ says to us, "In this way — through this washing with water — I will come to you and give you a share in my death and resurrection." How important that he should command us. How important that it should be clear that this baptism in no way depends on us. That it isn't just a bright idea of ours.

We might meet God everywhere, of course. But for precisely that reason he is hard to find anywhere in particular. We may seek him in nature or within our own spirits. But even if he is there, we will find him shrouded in darkness — the darkness that is our own spirit, the darkness that is his own immensity.

How important, therefore, that connected with the water of baptism there should also be a word of command. The God whom we might meet everywhere and who, therefore, is hard to find anywhere in particular — this God has said he will meet us in this particular place, in the water of baptism. Even in the command there is hidden that promise: Do this, and I will be present as the crucified and risen One.

The word of God we hear in baptism is not only command, then, but also promise. Promises are, of course, very familiar to us. We make them every day. But stop and think about the promises we make each other. Every one of them has conditions attached, even those we try to make unconditionally. For behind all our promises must stand at least this one unspoken condition: I will do this — unless I die. I can keep the promise only if I'm still alive. Only if death has not taken me. And no matter how faithful we are, it is therefore likely to be true of us that some day we will make a promise we cannot keep. We'll just run out of time.

The one thing we cannot promise is that part of the future which will not be ours to possess or give. At some point for each of us that future we would like to promise we will not have. It's a simple fact, and that unspoken condition lies behind every promise we make, and behind every promise the little gods of our world make — a point nicely made by William F. May about the rituals connected to a military funeral. "The casket of a soldier is draped with his country's flag, but when the coffin is about to be lowered into the ground, the flag is neatly folded and withdrawn. At the last moment, if you will, it betrays him." There is the poignancy and pain of human life, the unspoken condition behind every human promise.

But not behind the promise God has made us in our baptism. His is an unconditional promise; for it is spoken by Christ, who was placed into the grave but who now stands beyond death. In our baptism we are lowered into that grave with him, and St. Paul draws the only possible conclusion: "If we have been united with him in a death like his, we shall certainly be united with him in a resurrection like his."

The unspoken condition that haunts every promise we make does not haunt this promise. The "faithful cross" is a sign of triumph. Jesus is master even of death. He can promise unconditionally.

How can water do such great things? It is not the water indeed that does them, but the word of God which is in and with the water. A word that takes matters out of our own hands and points simply to the command in which God commits himself to cleanse us in the baptismal water. A word which promises that, since we have been united with Christ in death, we are quite right to prepare, to wait, and to hope for Easter — his Easter, but also ours.

3. Faith

> For if we have been united with him in a death like his,
> we shall certainly be united with him in a resurrection
> like his. We know that our old self was crucified with him
> so that the sinful body might be destroyed, and we might
> no longer be enslaved to sin. For he who has died is freed
> from sin. But if we have died with Christ, we believe that
> we shall also live with him.
>
> ROMANS 6:5-8

In the past two weeks we have explored the significance of
baptism as water and word: a washing with water, carried out
in obedience to the command of Christ, and to which is attached the promise of Christ. We have seen that this is not
merely some abstract teaching, some matter for thought
only; for, as Paul makes very clear in Romans 6, this washing
with water makes us participants in the death of Christ and
promises unconditionally that we will share his resurrected
life. The movement in baptism is from the old age of sin and

death into which we are born to the new age of promise, which Christ even now lives as the first fruits of those who are to follow. That is to say, the movement in baptism is from Lent to Easter. It is, therefore, no accident or misunderstanding that we should make baptism our theme during Lent. The misunderstanding would occur, rather, if we failed to see how closely connected they are in the Christian life and the life of the church.

But there is more to be said about baptism than that it is water + word. Last week we noted the question in the *Small Catechism* in which Luther makes explicit the connection of water and word in baptism. *How can water do such great things?* he asks. But last week, concentrating as we were upon the command and the promise of the word attached to the water, I read only a part of Luther's answer to that question: *It is not the water indeed that does them, but the word of God which is in and with the water. . . .* Today, though, we complete the sentence: *It is not the water indeed that does them, but the word of God which is in and with the water, and faith, which trusts such word of God in the water.*

The word of promise both calls for and makes possible the response of faith. What else could we possibly say during Lent, during a time when the One we call "Lord" can be seen only as a man of sorrows? The Christian life into which we are baptized is, from beginning to end, a pilgrimage made in faith: "the conviction of things not seen," as the writer of Hebrews puts it. This is just as clear in Romans 6. Paul stressses (in v. 4) that, just as Christ was raised from the dead, so we who have been baptized into Christ should even now walk in newness of life. Yet, that new life, though ours in Christ, still has about it something of a hidden character. It is still marked by the words "not yet," is still an object of promise, still calls for faith, not sight.

Twice in the few verses from Romans that we read today St. Paul makes clear that the new life is ours in hope — that we believe what we have not yet fully experienced. "For if we have been united with Christ in a death like his," he writes in verse 5, "we shall certainly be united with him in a resurrection like his." The new life is ours; yet Easter is still to come for us. And again in v. 8: "if we have died with Christ, we believe that we shall also live with him." Baptism is not a ticket to a triumphant life in which faith is no longer needed; baptism is permission to trust and entrance into a life of trust.

How can water do such great things? It is not the water indeed that does them, but the word of God which is in and with the water, and faith, which trusts such word of God in the water. Permission to trust — that is what your baptism means.

To see this — really to see it — is to be delivered from puzzles we sometimes find in baptism. We wonder about baptizing infants, puzzling over how they can possibly have faith. And we strain for answers when others object to such a practice. Infants, we say, are part of "all nations," and Jesus says to baptize all nations. True enough. But it is as if we have forgotten that the whole of the baptized life from start to finish is a life of faith — a life of trust in what we can neither see nor fully comprehend. As if the very best image we could find of such trust in ordinary life were not that of a baby in the arms of its mother — uncomprehending, but secure. We talk as if the marvel and mystery of baptism were that a baby should be able to believe like an adult. Whereas the real marvel and mystery — the mystery of grace — is that in baptism we should receive permission to trust, to be as "newborn babes," and to believe what we do not see.

Faith trusts the word of God in the water. Faith, therefore, conforms the whole of our life to the essential pattern of Lent. Jesus sets his face steadfastly toward the cross, he commits his spirit into the hands of his Father, and believes what cannot be seen: that the Father will not fail to vindicate him even in the darkness of death. Just so, we move through life trusting the promise that for us too a new birth is hidden with Christ under the cross. We say with St. Paul of our baptized lives: "if we have died with Christ, we believe that we shall also live with him." Faith trusts the word of God in the water of baptism — and faith alone makes possible the movement from Lent to Easter.

4. Forgiveness

We know that our old self was crucified with him so that the sinful body might be destroyed, and we might no longer be enslaved to sin. For he who has died is freed from sin.

ROMANS 6:6-7

What is Lent about? The hymn captures at least one aspect of Lent's significance:

> O Lord, throughout these forty days
> You prayed and kept the fast;
> Inspire repentance for our sin,
> And free us from our past.

We have talked of water and word, which make baptism the gift it is. We have spoken of faith, which receives the gift in baptism. Now it is time to emphasize the theme to which that hymn verse points: forgiveness. Freedom from the dead hand of the past. We are buried with Christ, Paul says, that we might no longer be enslaved to sin. One who has died is freed from sin. If Jesus means freedom, the darkness of sin cannot overcome the light that shines from the empty tomb, bringing forgiveness and release from old guilts and failures. When we were baptized and set apart as God's people, we were baptized into Christ. St. Paul therefore concludes of us: "He who has died is freed from sin."

Luther concluded the same in his *Small Catechism*. *What does baptism give or profit?* he asked. *It works forgiveness of sins, delivers from death and the devil, and gives eternal salvation to all who believe this, as the words and promises of God declare.* In baptism we find God's favor in the Christ who is for us even in our sin. We find a grace that is pardon and that frees from sin.

Perhaps some of you have read the Chronicles of Narnia by C. S. Lewis — stories for children about the marvelous land of Narnia, stories at least as good for adults. In one of those stories, *The Voyage of the Dawn Treader,* a boy named Eustace — who's not a very nice boy — is turned into a dragon when he falls asleep in a cave, lying on a dragon's hoard of treasure, and thinking greedy, dragonish thoughts. Some time later, when Eustace has almost despaired of ever being cured, he meets Aslan by night — Aslan, the great lion who is creator of Narnia and son of the Emperor beyond the sea — and Aslan tells him that the pain he suffers can be eased if he will bathe in the well nearby. Eustace is at once ready to do so, but Aslan tells him that he must first undress — that is, scratch off his scaly skin.

Eustace scratches and scrapes until his skin is peeled off, but just when he is ready to step into the water he looks down and sees that his foot is every bit as rough and wrinkled and scaly as it had been before. He isn't discouraged, though. He decides that he must have had another smaller, scaly skin underneath, and it too must be scratched away. And he does that — only to find, as he is preparing to step into the water, that there's still another skin underneath. So for the third time he scratches and claws his way out of his skin — only to find yet another underneath.

And then the lion speaks: "You will have to let me undress you." The first tear the lion makes goes so deep that it seems to Eustace to have pierced to the heart. And when the lion begins to tear off the skin, it hurts worse than anything Eustace has ever felt. But the lion persists, pulls off the thick skin that Eustace could never have gotten off, and throws Eustace into the water.

Suddenly Eustace is a boy again — no longer a dragon. Try as often as he might, Eustace could not have turned himself from a dragon into the boy he was meant to be. He had to entrust himself to the lion, permit the lion to cut to the very heart — and to throw him into what we can only call a baptismal water. Eustace had to die to his own dragonish self in order to be a boy again. For, as St. Paul says, "he who has died is freed from sin."

Baptismal grace is cleansing grace. It may hurt; it cuts to the heart. But that cleansing grace is forgiveness. It is pardon. It is baptism into the Christ who is for us. The truth about ourselves is the truth Eustace discovered: try as we might we cannot get to the bottom of the sin that has us in its grip, cannot free ourselves from the old guilts that haunt and paralyze us. For we can never on our own find the perspective from which to see ourselves whole and be sure that the wrinkles and scales have all been scratched away.

Because we cannot, the lion of Judah must baptize, must inspire repentance for our sin and free us from our past. What we cannot even fully see, he must pardon. When we are more dragonish than human, he must continue to be for us. When we are burdened with that self which we can neither accept nor get rid of, he must peel it off and take us into his grave, so that the one who has died with him can be free from sin. The grace of baptism is — and must be — pardon. The Christ of baptism is Christ for us. And the forgiveness of baptism — a washing that frees us from sin by burying us with Christ — is the only way by which we can come through Lent to Easter.

5. Life

What shall we say then? Are we to continue in sin that
grace may abound? By no means! How can we who died
to sin still live in it? Do you not know that all of us who
have been baptized into Christ Jesus were baptized into
his death? We were buried therefore with him by baptism
into death, so that as Christ was raised from the dead by
the glory of the Father, we too might walk in newness of
life. For if we have been united with him in a death like
his, we shall certainly be united with him in a resurrection like his. We know that our old self was crucified with
him so that the sinful body might be destroyed, and we
might no longer be enslaved to sin. For he who has died is
freed from sin. But if we have died with Christ, we believe
that we shall also live with him. For we know that Christ
being raised from the dead will never die again; death no
longer has dominion over him. The death he died he died
to sin, once for all, but the life he lives he lives to God. So
you also must consider yourselves dead to sin and alive to
God in Christ Jesus.

ROMANS 6:1-11

During these weeks of Lent we have reflected upon the first eleven verses of Romans chapter six. Those verses are certainly the most important biblical text for understanding the significance of baptism. We have found in them guidance to think about the water and word of baptism, about faith which trusts the promise of baptism, and about the forgiveness given in baptism when we are buried with Christ. But finally now, as we consider once more all eleven verses, it should become clear that their most fundamental theme has to do with the connection between baptism and life.

In his *Small Catechism* Luther uses four questions with their brief answers to discuss the significance of baptism for Christian faith and life. In previous weeks we have called to mind what he says in answer to the first three of those questions: *What is baptism? What does baptism give or profit?* and *How can water do such great things?* Up to now, however, we have said nothing about the fourth question, the one in which Luther draws a specific connection to Romans 6.

What does such baptizing with water signify? he asks. And answers: *It signifies that the old Adam in us should by daily contrition and repentance be drowned and die with all sins and evil lusts; and again, a new man daily come forth and arise, who shall live before God in righteousness and purity forever.*

Baptism means new life. In part that means, as we emphasized last week, the promise of new life — of Easter — hidden with Christ under the cross. It means forgiveness: grace as *pardon*, made ours by the Christ who is *for* us. As the hymn puts it:

Drawn to the cross, which Thou hast blest
With healing gifts for souls distrest,

To find in thee my life, my rest,
Christ Crucified, I come.

But this new life also means *power* — the power of Christ *in* us, the power to live that life of daily contrition and repentance of which Luther speaks. As, after all, the hymn also says:

And then for work to do for thee,
Which shall so sweet a service be
That angels well might envy me,
Christ Crucified, I come.

We come during Lent — we come right now — for pardon, but also for power. Power to live as new people.

Repentance and rededication are themes that get special attention during the season of Lent, a season we call "penitential." The hymns of Lent regularly call to mind the passion of Christ and our sin, which necessitated that passion. The narrative of the passion sets before us a figure like Peter who, having denied Christ, repented and wept bitterly. The whole of the season is marked by the call of the prophet Joel, heard on Ash Wednesday: "'Yet even now,' says the Lord, 'return to me with all your heart.'"

This is the theme of Lent, but not only of Lent. It is the theme of the entire Christian life. When Martin Luther nailed his 95 theses to the door of the castle church in Wittenberg, he wanted to find a way to make clear that the Christian life was not just an initial grace given in baptism, followed by our own struggle to overcome the past sins that still cling to us. He wanted, instead, to say that the entire

Christian life is empowered by God, is a never-ending return to the grace once given in baptism and still the motive force by which we live. And so, the first of his theses was a ringing declaration: "When our Lord and Master Jesus Christ said 'repent!' he willed the entire life of believers to be one of repentance." The theme of Lent is the theme of all Christian living; for the theme of Lent is cross and resurrection, pardon and the power for new life.

What does it mean to reclaim our baptism day by day? It means, as St. Paul says, to consider ourselves dead to sin and alive to God in Christ Jesus. When we say not simply "I was baptized," but, rather, "I am baptized," we claim the power of Christ for our lives, we commit ourselves to daily repentance. We set our face against the sin that still draws us, that is all around us and lies near at hand in the everyday worlds we inhabit — and we bury all that with Christ, reclaiming the baptismal grace that is the power of Christ in us.

In this way the whole of life can be seen as a Lenten season, marked by repentance and the cross — while, nonetheless, each new day can also carry the power of Easter, can become a day on which the water of our baptism renews and empowers us. Day by day, day after day, the new self can live — live as God wills, live before God in righteousness and purity forever.

> Be with us through this season, Lord,
> And all our earthly days.
> That when the final Easter dawns,
> We join in heaven's praise.

II. The Bonds of Life:
Sermons on the Decalog

The Ten Commandments have been an important source for Christian reflection on the moral life. They are not, however, easy to preach about — at least, not for me. My attempt was helped immeasurably when I learned from Karl Barth to see the promise buried in the command: the promise that God will make of us what he demands of us. To see that is to be able to make our own St. Augustine's constant refrain in Book 10 of his *Confessions:* "Give what you command, and command what you will." It was offensive to Pelagius then, and it would no doubt be offensive to his successors today, but it is the right way to approach the Decalog.

As to the content of the commandments, much of it could, no doubt, be known equally well through the light of reason. In that sense the Decalog largely recapitulates the natural law. Its injunctions must be heeded by any society that is to survive and flourish, though I have not tried to work out that point systematically in these sermons. But once we set the commandments also in the context of the promise of God's grace in Christ, we may find in them newer and richer meanings. In particular, we are likely to emphasize, as Luther so often does, not only their negative prohibitions but also the works of love they urge upon us. More problematically, we may also be faced with the tension between the tables of the law, a tension that cannot be fully overcome in human history.

The idea of structuring the content of the second table of the law in terms of five bonds I owe to a book I once used for teaching a children's catechetical class. The book, its title long since forgotten by me, has lived on in my memory only in this way. I am conscious of Barth's influence (*Church Dogmatics*, III/4) on my treatment of the family bond and of the influence of William F. May's *A Catalogue of Sins* in several of these sermons. There are marks of Josef Pieper's *The Four Cardinal Virtues*, and the impact of C. S. Lewis, evident at several places, is no doubt present at others where it may not be as readily apparent. Throughout, I have consulted Luther's catechisms.

6. The Family Bond

*Honor your father and your mother, so that you may live
long in the land the LORD your God is giving you.*

Finding guidance in the Bible for our lives is not as simple or
uncomplicated as sometimes thought, but there are a few
time-honored places to begin. One such place is the Decalog.
Time and again Christians have turned to it for help in dis-
covering what it might mean to live as God's people and followers of Jesus. In particular, the Ten Commandments have
played an important role in catechetical instruction. And so,
for the next six weeks we will turn to the Decalog for guidance. We will spend five weeks on the second table of the law
— those commandments that teach the meaning of love for
the neighbor. And then one week on the first table of the law
— on the command to love God above all else.

In doing this we are faithful to the words of Moses to Israel: "Fix these words of mine in your hearts and minds." In

doing this we also take seriously Jesus' word that the good tree must bear good fruit. Yet, we do this not because we seek an achievement in which we can boast before God, but because we know, as Paul says in Romans, that the righteousness of God has been manifested in Jesus Christ apart from the law — and that our boasting is in him.

In the numbering used by Lutherans there are seven commandments in the second table of the law, but, really, they concern themselves with five important bonds of human life:

- the family bond — in the command to honor one's parents
- the marriage bond — in the commandment forbidding adultery
- the life bond — in the commandment forbidding murder
- the property bond — in the commands forbidding theft and covetousness
- the speech bond — in the command forbidding slander and lying

In one way or another these five bonds are always important in human life. Any society and any culture will have to attend to them. The commandments recognize this; they point our attention to these bonds because in them human lives necessarily intersect.

This is clear in the fourth commandment, with which we begin today, the commandment that directs us to sustain the family bond. Our lives are always bound together through the process of human generation. And this is the first commandment with a promise. "Honor your father and your mother, so that you may live long in the land the LORD your God is giving you." We may think of this as a promise to individuals — and then wonder why things don't always seem to turn out this way. Why the dutiful child doesn't always live a long and prosperous life. But that's not quite what the promise means. It is a statement of fact about human communities more than it is a reward for individual good behavior. For the commandment points us to a bond that must be sustained in any healthy society. Where there is no willingness to honor parents, no reverence for the sacrifices ancestors made on our behalf — in that sort of society, who will want to bear and rear children? Who will want to sacrifice for the sake of future generations if that sacrifice is not honored?

The Latin word the Romans used for this reverential spirit was *pietas* — piety. Piety toward those who had nourished one's life. No community can be healthy without such piety. And when we understand the promise in this way — understand that human life is so structured — we may well fear for our own communities. Communities in which parents in particular and those who are older in general are often without honor. In which the point of life is always to be independent and to acknowledge as seldom as possible the sacrifices others have made for us.

What does it mean to be a child — living within the family bond? Quite clearly, it means different things at different stages of life. My relation to my parents is and should be very different now than when I was eighteen. And at eighteen it was quite different than at eight. But whatever our age, to be the child of our parents, to have been raised and cared for by them, means to have received life as a free gift. In that way the parent really does stand in place of God — and really does deserve honor.

Suppose you wanted to repay your parents for the gift of life, how could you do it? How could you ever get back to the point where your existence was independent of theirs and you could start on equal terms with them? That point just doesn't exist. As children within a family bond, as those who even when adult are still children of parents, we are always people who have received a gift we had done nothing to deserve. We were needy — and they cared for us. They stood in God's place, shared in his creative role as givers of life. The debt we owe them cannot be repaid. All we can do is what the commandment calls upon us to do: we can honor them as those God chose to give us life.

If we do so honor them, to the degree that we do it, we have nothing to boast of. For we do no more than seek, in our halting way, not to refuse the grace of God which has been revealed in Jesus, the Son of the Father. If we receive life from our parents with gratitude, we do what the Son of the Father has done from eternity. We conform to the pattern of his Sonship.

What does it mean to be a parent — living within the family bond? It means, as Karl Barth puts it, the honor of standing as God's representative to our children. The obligation of caring for and training those children. But it also means danger. For in this godlike responsibility there are great temptations. The temptation to exercise a tyrannical authority — to forget to be as gracious as the heavenly Father is. But perhaps even more — the temptation to think, and hope, and act as if we could really protect our children from the sorrows and sufferings of life. To forget that in baptism we have handed them over into the keeping of a greater Father. To forget that every time we pray for them we are recognizing our own frailty, our own inability to be the parent they ultimately need.

We cannot, finally, be their protectors. We can only be witnesses — standing before our children in the confidence that God is the One who undertakes to care for them, that he must be their protector and guardian, the only One who can truly live *for* them. It is the honor and obligation of a parent to be such a witness. No more than that. But also no less than that high honor.

And in all this — in our lives as children and as parents, we may fail as often as we succeed. The mistakes we easily forgive in the neighbor's children we cannot tolerate in our own. The frailties in others which evoke our sympathy we resent in our own parents. Nor is this at all surprising. It is not surprising that children should resent their parents almost as much as they love them; for it is no easy thing to know that we are forever indebted, in a way we cannot repay, to our parents for the gift of life. It is not surprising that parents should sometimes seem to smother their children — so strong is the impulse to protect.

Yet it is here, if anywhere — within the family bond — that we begin to learn the movements of the dance of love, a life marked by giving and receiving. Here our self-interested impulses are disciplined, our desire for independence controlled. As children we must gradually learn to receive love, to acknowledge dependence without resenting it. As parents we must learn to give love without seeking to possess forever the one we love.

And when we fail — as we often must — we can only turn to the one child who can stand before the heavenly Father as justified by his deeds, the one child who has kept this commandment. We can find in him the way to the Father — the only Father who has been utterly faithful to his wayward children. And, parents and children together, we must confess our failure to honor this Father by living in love within the family bond. And we must ask him to begin to reshape us into the form of his own love, so that we may live long in the land he will give us.

7. The Marriage Bond

You shall not commit adultery.

EXODUS 20:14

A very simple and straightforward text, isn't it? Rather elegant in its straightforwardness and simplicity: You shall not commit adultery. Yet, I venture to say, it's not a text often preached on. Indeed, in recent years something rather strange has been happening to the church's approach to marriage. On the one hand, couples who wish to be married are often required by pastors to attend a number of counseling sessions in advance so that their motives and fitness for marriage, their readiness and their maturity, may be probed. Yet, in these very same years the church's public teaching about marriage has been virtually nonexistent. *Private* discussion and counsel. *Public* silence.

In private discussion and counsel we need only help the couple desiring marriage to probe their own understandings, explore together their own concerns. But in public teaching

we may be more responsible to speak an authoritative word —
a word which suggests that the marriage bond is not ours to
do with as we please. And indeed, many church members today think their marriages are none of the church's business.
They want to be married in church, but not in anything that
very closely resembles a worship service. They don't want
their understanding of marriage questioned. If at some future
date they decide to end their marriage, that's no concern of the
pastor. He ought simply hold himself in readiness to perform
another ceremony should either of them wish to remarry.

The seventh stanza from Luther's hymn on the Decalog
sounds rather quaint in such a world.

> Be faithful to thy marriage vows,
> Thy heart give only to thy spouse;
> Thy life keep pure, and lest thou sin,
> Use temperance and discipline.

The hymn outlines standards to which we are to hold each
other. It enunciates virtues — temperance and discipline —
which we are to nurture. It doesn't think of marriage as a
purely private matter. Likewise, the sixth commandment exists to remind us that the marriage bond is far too important
in human life to be the private concern of two individuals
alone.

Why? What about this bond is so important that one of
the commandments should call upon us to sustain it? "Sex is
a natural function, just like breathing," some will say. "We
just need to learn to treat it naturally, to get over our hang-ups
and our embarrassment about it. We need to stop imagining
that it's especially bad."

Notice the assumption: that what seems natural for human beings needs no control. That what comes naturally to us is good if we will just let it alone. But think about that. The desire to live is quite natural to human beings; yet we may need the command that forbids us to live by murdering others. The desire to possess is natural to human beings; yet we may need the commandments forbidding theft and covetousness.

Without such control, injustice runs wild in human life. Without such control, selfishness becomes destructive. And the same is true of the sphere of life governed by the sixth commandment. Sexual desires are not worse or more impure than any other desires. But they are equally subject to distortion. They too need control — temperance and discipline, as the hymn put it. In this sphere of life also selfishness may overcome us. We may think only of ourselves and not of our commitments to others. We may want that to which we have no right. We may want it even if the harm done to others is enormous.

Unchastity — another quaint old word — is rooted in selfishness and leads to injustice. People get hurt. Confidences are betrayed. Expectations are disappointed. And all of this may seem quite "natural," of course. But, natural or not, it is harmful and destructive. So the commandment exists to issue a warning. To point to the fact that the sexual impulse must be controlled and disciplined, lest the private vice of selfishness lead to the public sin of injustice.

All this, however, captures only the negative reason for the commandment protecting the marriage bond. When in his *Small Catechism* Luther explained the sixth commandment, he put it positively: *We should fear and love God that we may lead a chaste and decent life in word and deed, and each love and honor his spouse.*

We have seen that the family bond is one through which God is at work in us, shaping our love after the pattern of his own. Teaching parents to give freely; teaching children to receive without resentment. And the sixth commandment, like the fourth, has such a concern. The other commandments in the second table of the law treat our relation to more distant neighbors, to any neighbor at all. But the family bond and the marriage bond concern very near neighbors — the parent, the child, the spouse. In these near neighbor bonds God works on us, seeks to make us people who really know know how to love.

In the Bible, marital imagery is often used to picture the relation of God and his people. Israel is called to be God's covenant partner. Yahweh is lover, bridegroom, husband of his people. And however often Israel may be unfaithful to her promise, God does not forget his covenant. In the New Testament the church is the bride of Christ, who is the faithful lover. And that faithfulness of Christ to his church — faithfulness even to death on a cross — becomes the standard by which faithfulness of husband and wife is measured, and the pattern which their love ought to reenact.

"You shall not commit adultery." That commandment exists not only to prohibit something but to point toward a great good. You shall not be like unfaithful Israel, like our wayward congregations of Christians. You shall be like faithful Yahweh, faithful Christ — who never defects from his promise.

When we give ourselves sexually, we give *ourselves*. Not just a passing pleasure. Not just a moment of life, but our-

34

selves. And therefore, sexual commitment is not to be separated from a sharing of the whole of life — not if we want the great good of faithfulness to come to its fruition in our lives. We cannot give ourselves fully if we withhold the future; for then our commitment is not as full and complete as Christ's commitment to his church.

To see this, to see the positive good of faithfulness toward which the commandment points, is to see that this commandment is directed to all of us. Unmarried and married. Young and old. All are called to faithfulness.

Are you young, and wanting to know what to do to prepare yourself for marriage some day? Well then, pay less attention to all the advice the books give. Instead, practice making promises and keeping them. Learn to be faithful now.

Are you older, and perhaps not as likely any longer to marry? Or once married but now widowed? Still, though, within the church, the bride of Christ. And still, therefore, needing to learn the meaning of faithful love in the whole of life — a lesson God may choose to teach some of us through ways other than the marriage bond.

Are you divorced? Then do not be afraid to name your failure and to measure it by the standard of God's own faithfulness; for in just that measure he continues faithful to you. He never forsakes his covenant.

After all, the story the Bible tells is the long story of a marriage: Israel, an unfaithful bride, lusting after the gods of other nations. Yahweh, everlastingly faithful to his covenant promise. To understand the sixth commandment we must set it into that larger context. We must hear it as part of the story the Bible tells.

"You shall not commit adultery." It sounds simply like a

command. But not within the larger story. Place it within the whole narrative, and we cannot miss the hint of promise that lies buried there. You *shall not* commit adultery. You *shall* be faithful. That is a promise. For the faithful God, the One who never fails to keep covenant, is at work in us and our history, making us what we are not yet: faithful lovers. And at the very end of the story the Bible tells, when the seer in Revelation peers in vision into the future, he sees the completion of God's work. He beholds a new heaven and earth, and the new Jerusalem "prepared as a bride beautifully dressed for her husband." He hears a voice saying, "Now the dwelling of God is with men, and he will live with them."

Our task in the meantime is to let our lives and, if we are married, our marriages reflect the faithfulness of Christ to his bride — trusting the promise buried in the command and spelled out in the story, the promise that the God who keeps covenant will make of us what we are not yet and will not fail to prepare the wedding banquet.

8. The Life Bond

You shall not murder.

EXODUS 20:13

The fourth commandment and the sixth commandment, which we considered the past two weeks, protect and sustain bonds of life that involve us closely and intimately. Our marriages and our families are flesh-and-blood attachments. There's nothing abstract about them; on the contrary, they constitute the air we breathe every day.

By contrast, the bond to which the fifth commandment points — the simple tie that joins together every human being in our shared nature and life — may seem more abstract. Because it is universal, because it involves us everywhere we turn, it may seem to be nowhere in particular. It lacks the specificity that family and marriage have. What we encounter everywhere we may tend to take for granted.

But the fifth commandment reminds us that we dare not. That we dare not fail to see in every human face the fellow human being, the neighbor, the one whom Christ loves. When God made his covenant with Noah and his sons after the great flood, he gave them all the animals of the earth as food for them to eat. The blood of the animal could be shed that human beings might live. But not so the blood of a fellow human. They were not to live off each other. God tells Noah that he will demand of us an account of the life of our fellows. "Whoever sheds the blood of man, by man shall his blood be shed; for God made man in his own image."

If you have ever read the memoirs of soldiers or the accounts of men in battle, you sometimes get a sense of this common humanity when a soldier recounts the first time he ever took the life of an enemy soldier. Quite often, even here when the killing may be justified, there is a terrifying sense of awe — the sense that he has not just killed an enemy soldier, but someone like himself, with whom he is joined in the common bond of life. And perhaps the worst thing about war is not that some are killed but that it may blind us to the human face the enemy shares with us.

When we want to make this point today, we're likely to use the language of "rights" and say that every individual has human rights. That's not, however, the language the Bible uses. Its language is that of the image of God in which we share, of human beings as those who receive life as a loan from God. And what we are to respect and protect in the fellow human being is the gift God has made him — the gift of a time and a place — a time and a place which we did not give and which we are not to take.

Indeed, the Bible goes still farther. The respect and protection we owe the human being who shares God's image with us becomes something more than just respect when we remember that in the incarnation God takes our life into his own. He becomes one of us and shares in our common bond of life. God stands by the human being — and respect is transformed into love, and protection into concern. In the face of the other person we now see not just the face of a fellow human being made like us in God's image — we see also the face of Christ.

The commandment forbids murder of that one whom Christ loves. That is, it forbids not all killing — since there may be killing by a policeman or a soldier which is not murder — but it forbids killing which fails to see the image of God in the enemy and is not limited by such vision. It forbids killing in which hatred plays any part — and, indeed, as Jesus makes clear in the Sermon on the Mount, forbids not just the killing but the hatred alone. And, as William May once noted, it forbids hatred in all its manifestations: The hatred which as anger is directed toward past quarrels and arguments. The hatred which as suspicion is directed toward the future. The hatred which as resentment of another is directed toward the present and poisons life. Anger, suspicion, resentment — all destroy the bond of life we share with our fellow human beings.

Because the neighbor is made in God's image, the commandment forbids such actions and attitudes. And because in the neighbor we see the face of Christ, the commandment does more than just forbid; it calls for active love and concern for our neighbors. Luther captures that positive thrust in the *Small Catechism*'s explanation of the fifth commandment: *We should fear and love God that we may not hurt nor harm our neighbor in his body, but help and befriend him in every bodily need.* Thus, we break this commandment not only by hatred of the neighbor in all its forms, but also by neglect of our neighbors — by failing to help and befriend them where and when we are able.

We might, in fact, say that there is something even worse in neglect than in hatred. When I hate an enemy, he at least has my attention. I at least take him into account and recognize his concerns — if only to oppose them. But the person whom I neglect, whose needs I just fail to see, might as well not exist. That's how little he counts for in my world. For this is what neglect means: that we can choose not to enter into the world of the neighbor in need, choose not to see his need, choose not to help and befriend her in every bodily need. And then, too, the commandment is broken. Then we hurry along the other side of the road with the priest and Levite who did not see the beaten man as a fellow human being joined with them in a shared bond of life.

Sometimes, it is true, neglect may be the best we can manage. We may deal with our hatred of the enemy by pushing him from our consciousness — and thus use one vice to control another. But even if this may work to some extent, it is not the way we Christians are counseled to take. "To thy foe do thou good," Luther's hymn on the Decalog says. And Jesus calls on us to love the enemy. Not to forget the enemy, but to seek to make of that enemy a friend.

For is this not the Christian gospel? That God has come to live as one of us and that — as Paul puts it in Romans 5 — he has come as One with whom we were enemies. While we were enemies, he came to be reconciled. He comes as One who angers us by his judgment of us. As One of whom we are suspicious when he asks that we entrust our lives to him. As One whose claims to control our life we resent. As One we would be glad to ignore. Recognizing him as the enemy, we crucify him. And yet, it is the mystery of God's grace that we should learn to love this enemy whom we murdered.

If this enemy is for us, who can be against us? If this enemy does not strike back, if he continues to side with us, then we have learned what it means to be loved with God's love. If in every enemy we see the face of Christ whom we have come to love, then what enemies can remain for us?

We have a long way to go until we live in such a world, until a day when our vision will be that clear — so unclouded by sin that we no longer see any enemies. But we know that by God's grace it can and will be done. For we have begun to learn to love Jesus, who was our enemy but who stood by to help and befriend us in every bodily need. And, as St. Paul writes, we can be confident that the God who has begun this good work in us will carry it on to completion until the day of Jesus Christ.

9. The Property Bond

*You shall not steal. . . . You shall not covet your neigh-
bor's house. You shall not covet your neighbor's wife or
his manservant or maidservant, his ox or donkey, or anything that belongs to your neighbor.*

EXODUS 20:15, 17

In the book *Perelandra,* one of the space fantasies by C. S.
Lewis, a man named Ransom is magically taken from our
earth to the planet of Perelandra, a newly created world of almost indescribable beauty. Shortly after his arrival, Ransom
finds himself in a part of a wood where gourds of yellow fruit
hang from the trees. He is terribly thirsty, but he doesn't
know whether this fruit is harmful to human beings. So he
decides to take just one small "experimental" sip of the juice
from the fruit, but at the very first sip he forgets all caution.
The pleasure he gets from the fruit is so intense that he cannot even find words to describe it. At once Ransom drinks the
juice from the gourd and reaches to pick another. But sud-

denly he stops — realizing that he is no longer hungry or thirsty. He is drawn by the desire to repeat a pleasure so intense; yet something stops him.

A little later he has a similar experience with some trees he calls "bubble trees." These trees, it seems, draw up water from the ocean, enrich it in some way, and then produce little spheres that swell until, reaching a certain size, they burst and give off a delicious fragrance. Before Ransom has discovered the secret of the trees, he puts out his hand to touch one. At once — since he has popped one of the bubbles — he gets a little shower with that delicious fragrance. But now, realizing the nature of the trees, Ransom has a thought: Here is a large clump of trees. He could step back, take a running start, plunge through the trees popping many of the spheres at once, and have a marvelous experience. But again, something stops him. He reflects to himself:

> This itch to have things over again, as if life were a film that could be unrolled twice or even made to work backwards . . . was it possibly the root of all evil? No: of course the love of money was called that. But money itself — perhaps one valued it chiefly as a defence against chance, a security for being able to have things over again. . . .

Ransom has one more experience like this a little later. He finds some bushes which bear green berries that are good to eat. As he eats, though, Ransom discovers that a few of the berries have a bright red center and are especially tasty. The thought occurs to him that he could look only for those with the red center and throw the rest away. But again, something stops him even though, as he thinks to himself, in our world we'd call those special ones "redhearts" and learn how to breed and sell them for considerably more than the others.

What Ransom is getting on Perelandra is a lesson about things — and about the right attitude toward things. He is learning to receive with joy the gift that is given, and learning not to spoil that joy with a search for what is not given. The seventh, ninth, and tenth commandments — which forbid stealing and coveting — are also about things. About possessions.

We need these commandments. For if human life is bound together in families and marriages, and if all human beings share the bond of a life made in God's image, it is also true that our lives are joined by what we may call a property bond. Things, too, are important — because we need them to survive, because we need them for life to be full and satisfying, because we need them to serve our neighbors, because we are given dominion over the creation (which means, in part, over the world of things). No human society can get along without paying some attention to this bond, to the importance of possessions for our common life.

What do these commandments forbid? It's not altogether easy to say what stealing is. Here, as with so many other commandments, Luther's explanations suggest that we are forbidden not only to harm but also to fail to help the neighbor in need. *We should fear and love God that we may not take our neighbor's money or goods, nor get them by false ware or dealing, but help him to improve and protect his property and business.* And in his *Large Catechism* Luther gives an even broader definition. Stealing, he says, is "taking advantage of our neighbor in any sort of dealing that results in loss to him."

Listen to that definition again while thinking about the way we sell houses and cars, the way we advertise products, the way some people work at their jobs, the way business deals are sometimes struck. Stealing is "taking advantage of our neighbor in any sort of dealing that results in loss to him."

It is a serious question — and one to which there are few clear answers — how this commandment is to be applied in a society with an economy such as ours. But it is a question about which Christians need to think. Our economic life is founded upon transactions in which we seek a profit. And there is a line — but a very fine line indeed — between seeking a profit and seeking to take advantage of someone by means of a transaction that results in loss to him. Perhaps the best we can do when striking our deals is to keep in mind the Golden Rule: If the deal I am abut to strike with you is one that our world considers neither wrong nor unlawful, but if I know that it is a bargain I would feel cheated to have made were I in your place — then it's time to reconsider.

But the property bond involves more than just stealing — more than having and getting possessions. It involves attitudes. Hence, we have the commands forbidding covetousness. We covet when we desire the good things that are someone else's.

What, we might ask, is so bad about that? These things are good; the whole world is God's good creation. Why not want such good things for ourselves? It will not do to answer this question by denying what is true: that possessions are indeed good things, that they enrich human life and are given for our enjoyment. Nor will it do simply to pretend that contentment is the greatest of Christian virtues and that the poor

45

man should not also want some of the good things of life. Contentment is a virtue usually praised by the rich when speaking of the poor.

But still, there is something wrong with coveting. What is wrong is a simple matter of emphasis. It's not wrong that I want the neighbor's *goods;* it is wrong that I want *the neighbor's* goods. When I covet your good things, it's as if I blot out my own relation to God — the time and the place and the gifts given me. How, William May asks, can I say, "I wish I were in your shoes," while being grateful for the gifts God has given me? "I wish I were in your shoes." I wish, that is, that I were not the person I am. Blind to the treasures God has given me, I can only be angry that he has not made me you.

If it were just a matter of wanting the neighbor's *goods,* we would at least only be wanting what is good, things we lack and which it would be a blessing to have. But when we want *the neighbor's* goods, we not only blind ourselves to the gifts that are ours. We are also bothered that others have good things we lack. Soon it may be not our own ill fortune that concerns us, but another's good fortune. Soon we may prefer that neither of us should have a good thing than that the neighbor should have it and we should do without.

The desire to take advantage of others, dissatisfaction with our own gifts, mean-spiritedness at the good fortune of others — these are ways in which we break the commandments that relate to the bond of property in human life. And, we must admit, the actions and attitudes that break these commandments will not be overcome in our lives simply through sermons that urge us to be content with what we have. Even to say, as Luther does in his *Large Catechism,* "You have a rich lord; surely he is sufficient for your needs," will not by itself be enough. It takes more than words to root this sin out of our lives. It takes a deed.

For all of us are like Ransom on Perelandra — dominated to some extent by the itch to have things over again. By the desire to have things as a defense against chance, so that we can be master of our fate. Needing something we can trust, we are driven to try to take control. And it is a deed — God's deed — that sets us free from this desire.

God's deed in Christ — who, though he was rich, yet for our sakes became poor. Who, though he was in the form of God, did not count equality with God a thing to be grasped, but took upon himself the form of a servant. Rich and poor alike are needy before this God in whom the rich come to see their poverty and the poor their riches.

Why seek to stand in the shoes of another, when God has made himself present to us and set his hand upon us in our baptism? Why seek to keep every good thing under our own lock and key when the lord of the universe has broken the lock that kept him in the grave? The good deed that makes us all wealthy has been done. We have a share in Christ, a good thing that can never be exhausted and which no one need fear to share. And because the deed has been done, Luther's words can ring true: "You have a rich lord; surely he is sufficient for your needs."

10. The Speech Bond

You shall not give false testimony against your neighbor.

EXODUS 20:16

Dietrich Bonhoeffer is well known as a Lutheran theologian whose opposition to the Nazi regime led him to join first the Confessing Church in Germany and, then even, a resistance movement aiming to overthrow Hitler. Some of the letters and papers Bonhoeffer wrote while in prison before his execution have been widely read. In one of them, writing to his fellow conspirators, he looks forward to the end of the war and the need that will then arise to reconstruct German society once Hitler is gone. And he asks himself and his fellow conspirators, can we have any role to play in that movement of reconstruction and renewal? Or, as he put it, will we be of any use then? We who have had to learn to be devious and deceitful, will we be of any use when Germany once again needs honest, straightforward people? Will we be able to find our way out of the dark deceit and treachery of the revolutionary's world into the plain light of day in which honest citizens trust each other's word?

A tragic case — but a perceptive recognition of the place of speech in human society. The commandments remind us of the bonds of human life: that we are bound together with near neighbors in families and marriages, and bound together with still more distant neighbors in the common life we share, in the possessions we all need to live — and through the spoken word, without which there can be no life together.

It is so common and regular an occurrence that we forget the importance of speech in our lives. We wait anxiously and impatiently for a child to say that first word. We say "I love you," or "I promise you," or "I'll give you," or "I believe," or "I am dying," or "I forgive you." And even when we say none of these important words, we are constantly communicating — constantly bound together and in touch with each other through speech.

Because speech is so central in human life, it can be a powerful agent not only for good but also for evil. What is precious to you? Your family, your marriage, your life, your possessions. All of them. But also — your good name. And the eighth commandment exists to control human speaking, in order that no one's good name may be unjustly damaged.

In its most literal sense the eighth commandment emphasizes public testimony; it forbids slander and defamation of the neighbor. But, of course, it must also forbid lying and deceit; for in order to slander one person I must lie to another.

Everyone knows that it has always been difficult to be sure about what wrongful lying really involves. Perhaps you sometimes read Miss Manners' column in the newspaper. She claims to be dealing only in etiquette and not in morality, but on occasion she can also be a rather perceptive moralist. Once, replying to a question, she suggested a rather helpful distinction between "the truth, the whole truth, and nothing but the truth."

The whole truth is the moral answer to such questions as, "Did you take a cookie after I told you not to?" Such an answer might be, "No, but I ate the cooking chocolate." One must always speak the whole truth when morality is at stake.

Nothing but the truth is more useful on social occasions. For example: The question, "How do I look?" may be answered with, "To me, you're always beautiful," even though the whole truth would require adding, "but that dress makes you look like a truck."

The truth is the most complex concept of all. It means getting to the truth of the situation, rather than the crude literal surface truth. To answer the question, "Would you like to see some pictures of my grandchildren?" with the direct literal truth, "No! Anything but that!" would be cruel. But is that the real question? The real question, if one has any sensitivity to humanity, is, "Would you be kind enough to share some of my sentiments and reassure me that they are important and worthwhile?" to which a decent person can only answer, "I'd love to."

Now, that isn't bad, is it? To lie or to deceive the neighbor is not simply a matter of the words we use; it's a question of the truth we're trying to convey. When we are truthful, we don't just say a certain set of words; we speak in a way that says what we really mean and want. We do not use speech to construct a barrier between ourselves and the neighbor, but, instead, we use it to create a bond between us.

This means that here again — as with the other commandments — we are not just given a list of prohibited deeds. We are called to loving service in behalf of the neighbor. If love for the neighbor requires "nothing but the truth," we will look for a way to say it. If morality requires that "the whole truth" be spoken in order that another's good name be vindicated or in order that no one be deceived, we will speak up. And if — as will often be the case — getting at "the truth" of a situation requires more than just a form of words, we will look for words that get the job done. As Luther put it in explaining the eighth commandment, we will seek that truth which defends the neighbor's good name, speaks well of him, and puts the best construction on everything. The trick is not just to speak a certain way, but to want — really to want — what is good for our neighbors. And then, when we want that, perhaps it will be easier to find the truthful word that binds our lives together.

That is the meaning of truthfulness: harmony between our inner aims and our outer words, between what we want and what we say. Without such harmony we present a false image of who we are, and the other person, not knowing us as we really are, can establish no true bond with us.

Quite often we fail to achieve such harmony: When we boast, using words to conceal what we know deep inside to be the truth. When we make fun of what we don't have or can't have. When we speak insincerely in the hope of obtaining favors from others. When we slander a neighbor. Or possibly even — and this is why lying cannot be just a matter of the correct words — when we tell the truth about someone, but tell it in such a way, and at such a time, and to such a group of people, that his good name is harmed. In such moments we may seem to speak what is true, but we have not really served truth in our speaking. And we have not used speech in ways that will bind together our life, the life of the one about whom we speak, and the lives of those to whom we speak.

Truthfulness requires that harmony between inner and outer self — between what we want and what we say. To see this is to see why Jesus is called, not only the Way and the Life, but also the Truth. Jesus is the truthful revelation of God: the Word, the speech of God to us. What Jesus is, God is. If in Jesus we meet One who is merciful, then such mercy is God's true word to us. If in Jesus we find a faithful friend, then such faithfulness is the truth of God spoken to us. The God who is before and beyond and behind all else has revealed himself — spoken a true word — in Jesus, the child of Mary. He has bound himself to us through truthful speech. He has taken our side and vindicated our good name.

The word of God to us in Jesus is a word in which he binds himself to us. And the purpose of human speech is to reflect, however dimly, that word of God — to bind our lives together in harmony. The word of God to us in Jesus is a word that vindicates our good name and identifies with our cause. And the purpose of human speech is to reflect, however dimly, that word of God — to defend the cause of the needy and the innocent. The word of God to us in Jesus is a word which says what God really wants: that we should be his. And the purpose of human speech is to reflect, however dimly, that word of God — that we should learn to want what is good, so that our speaking may truly reflect our being. The word of God to us in Jesus is a word of blessing — the only blessing that gives life. And the purpose of human speech is to reflect, however dimly, that word of God — that we may be a blessing and speak God's blessing to others.

For it is his blessing that counts. The "well done" spoken by the Father to the Son on Easter morning — and the "well done" he will one day speak, and speak in truth, to all who bear the Son's name.

11. The Great Commandment

And one of them, a lawyer, asked Jesus a question, to test him. "Teacher, which is the great commandment in the law?" And he said to him, "You shall love the Lord your God with all your heart, and with all your soul, and with all your mind. This is the great and first commandment."

MATTHEW 22:35-38

If you were given the chance to preach just one sermon, you could do far worse than to take these words from Matthew's Gospel as your text. They direct our attention to the purpose and goal of human life: to our destiny as children who are to love their Father, a bride who is to love her bridegroom, creatures who are to love the Creator who has given them life and possessions, people whose final destiny is speech — to sing the praise of God.

For five weeks we have considered the commandments of the second table of the law, commandments that direct our attention to some of the important ways in which our lives are bound together. Today we consider the first table of the law not by thinking about the first three commandments in particular but simply by noting the summary of that first table which Jesus himself provides the lawyer who questions him. "You shall love the Lord your God with all your heart, and with all your soul, and with all your mind. This is the great and first commandment."

Although we know such passages well, we may not really talk much about love of God. We more readily may use the language of faith in God. And, as we will see, there is good reason for this. The more seriously we take the command to love God, the more earnestly we understand it as our created destiny, the more we will be driven to speak also of faith. Nevertheless, however much we may emphasize the language of faith, it is still true that love will abide when faith and hope are no longer needed. Christians are not wrong to pray in the words of the hymn:

> Oh, teach me, Lord, to love thee truly
> With soul and body, head and heart,
> And grant me grace that I may duly
> Practice fore'er love's sacred art.
> Grant that my every thought may be
> Directed e'er to thee.

But can this be? Is it possible that our "every thought" should be directed to God? There are, after all, two tables of the law summarized in the two commandments to love God and the neighbor. Sometimes the two may seem to coexist in perfect harmony: all other loves we receive with joy from God and offer back to him. Every thought directed toward God, not because we think of nothing else, but because all else is recognized as his gift and received with thanksgiving. But suppose this harmony does not exist. Suppose the two loves seem to clash. What then?

We get some sense of this possibility if we place side by side passages from consecutive chapters of Matthew's Gospel. In chapter eleven Jesus says: "Come to me, and I will give you rest. My yoke is easy and my burden light." But things sounded a bit different in chapter ten when that same Lord said: "I have not come to bring peace, but a sword. He who loves father or mother more than me is not worthy of me; he who loves son or daughter more than me is not worthy of me." There the burden of following Jesus hardly sounds light. What can Jesus mean by asking of his followers such renunciation? Can this be what the first and great commandment — love for God — requires?

We must understand the hard saying properly. As C. S. Lewis once noted, it is meant only for those who find it hard. For there can be no genuine renunciation if there is not first love. Lewis made the point by recalling a scene in Mauriac's *Life of Jesus* in which, when Jesus speaks of child against parent and parent against child, all the disciples are horrified — all except Judas, that is, who takes to the idea at once. The saying is not hard for him. Renunciation is not difficult unless first there is love, and he does not love.

So when Jesus suggests that the first and great commandment may mean even such renunciation, he does not mean that the whole of life is to be lived in this way, that we are to love nothing and no one except God. He means only, but he does surely mean, that disciples must always hold themselves in readiness for such renunciation — that we never know in advance what faithful love of God may ask of us. He means that the two great commandments, to love God and the neighbor, can be fully harmonized only at the end of history — and that, until then, faith is essential. We must learn to trust that the burden the Lord places upon us is light and his yoke easy.

Renunciation in the fullest sense, then, is not demanded of us every day. Of some of us, perhaps, it may never be demanded. Only God knows for certain what is needed on the path each of us takes to the day when we rest in him. Only God knows what renunciation of other good things is required to confirm our heart's love of him and make it steadfast.

But renunciation in a lesser sense is required of each of us — and is required day by day. Recall that the commandments of the second table point to what is precious in human life, what is worth loving. They also point, therefore, to those places in life where a kind of daily renunciation will be asked of us:

- The good name you have worked to maintain over the years is harmed by the gossip of others, but to defend it means seeking in turn to harm them — and renunciation is required.
- It's been a good year in your work, you've done well and are enjoying some of the good things of life, but it's evident that to continue such enjoyment will mean constant struggle and little rest. It's evident that you have begun to "need" more and more of those good things. And renunciation is required.

- On just the right kind of summer morning you feel once again the thrill of being alive, renewed energy and joy in life. But you cannot hold that moment forever. It passes into the heat of the day, which saps life and energy — a hint that renunciation is required.
- Your wedding anniversary rolls around and, taking time for a change to think about it, you are overwhelmed with a deep sense of love for your spouse. That love has grown with the years and made your heart glad. But you do not belong to each other forever; only till death parts you — and renunciation is required.
- You sit in the backyard watching your young children play and suddenly realize that this moment cannot be yours forever. It is their destiny to grow beyond dependence upon you. Yet, your heart wants to cling to the moment — and renunciation is required.

All these good gifts God gives us, and it would be wrong not to love them. Indeed, he binds our lives together in these ways so that our hearts may be trained in the movements of love. And the gifts are so good, the bonds of life so dear to us, that we are tempted to try to rest our heart in the gift and not in the Giver. The renunciation that is needed daily and is asked of each of us becomes a burden we do not want to bear, a cross we would rather not carry. To become lovers of God is a calling more strenuous than we sometimes desire. Perhaps it is not surprising, therefore, that often it is only suffering that turns us back to God, to the great and first command- ment. The little day-by-day renunciations are meant to teach us that God must be loved above all else — with our entire heart, soul, and mind. But the gifts are so good that we pass the lesson by until a renunciation that cannot be overlooked is asked of us — and we learn again that the heart can rest only in God.

In those moments especially — moments when it is hard to love God because the renunciation asked of us seems too great — in those moments more than any other faith becomes central in the Christian life. Faith that God is on our side and has shared our suffering. Faith that can endure the loss even of the most important bonds of human life — captured so nicely by Luther in his greatest hymn.

> And take they our *life,*
> *Goods, fame, child, and wife,*
> Let these all be gone,
> They yet have nothing won;
> The kingdom ours remaineth.

The five bonds that bring joy to us — even they are as nothing when set over against the kingdom.

When Jesus tells the lawyer that the first and great commandment is to love God with our whole heart, he is already on his way to the cross. This story comes in the twenty-second chapter of Matthew — after the Palm Sunday entrance into Jerusalem, and when Jesus is only days away from the demand to renounce all else out of love for his Father. The way of renunciation is not alien to God; he has gone that way before us and on our behalf.

Because he has, we can hear once more today the promise in the command. You *shall* love the Lord your God with all your heart, soul, and mind. You *shall* become a child who loves the Father, a bride eager to greet her bridegroom, a creature who loves the Creator from whom comes life and every good thing, a lover of God in whose speech the praise of God resounds. All that . . . you *shall* be.

And because by faith we trust that promise, we can even now begin to raise the song of praise which — when our love is perfected, our every thought directed to God, and faith replaced by sight — will be the anthem the new creation sings. Even then, perhaps, we may find no better words of praise than these:

God the Father, light-creator,
To thee laud and honor be.
To thee, Light of Light begotten,
Praise be sung eternally.
Holy Spirit, light-revealer,
Glory, glory be to thee.
Men and angels, now and ever
Praise the Holy Trinity.

III. Life in the Kingdom:
Sermons on the Sermon on the Mount

If we preach on the Decalog, we must sooner or later also preach on Matthew 5. Series A of the three-year lectionary gives us the opportunity to do so on four Sundays after the Epiphany. It is a good moment in the liturgical calendar to be invited or compelled to hear Jesus' words in Matthew 5, for it is a time when we can perhaps hear them not as harsh and strange commands but as a reflection of the divine glory that has entered our world at Bethlehem.

That, at least, is what I have tried to do in the four sermons that follow. The blessings which open the chapter must re-echo throughout the whole of it if we are to hear the gospel in Matthew 5. In certain respects my reading of this chapter, especially of its hard sayings, is an obviously Lutheran one. I distinguish what we may do on our own behalf from what we may do on behalf of a needy neighbor — a move I learned from a Methodist, Paul Ramsey, who had himself learned it from Luther. However, I read the "hard sayings" of Matthew 5 not only as an impossible demand, which exposes our need for pardon, but also as the promise of new birth in the Spirit of the risen Lord.

There is more to say about the Sermon on the Mount as a whole than I have said in these sermons on just one chapter of that sermon, but chapter five does, of course, contain some of the hardest of Jesus' hard sayings. If there is not in these sermons the specificity of those on the Decalog, there is probably greater struggle to understand the law in its relation to the gospel — a struggle which is lifelong and which preaching, in particular, can never for long evade.

12. The Blessing of the Kingdom

Charles Wesley wrote many beautiful and stirring hymns, but one of his greatest is surely "Love Divine, all love excelling/Joy of heav'n, to earth come down." What does it mean that Jesus should be Emmanuel, God with us? If the joy of heaven, God's love, has come down to earth, it means that the glory — the only glory that counts — has shined into our lives. "Fix *in us* thy humble dwelling," the hymn says. It is no small thing to ask God to dwell in us, to call upon God to let his glory possess us and control our thinking, saying, doing, and desiring. Think what we are asking of the Love Divine. "Finish, then, thy new creation/Pure and spotless let us be."

We ought to tremble at the thought: God's love actually committed to perfecting us. And it would, in truth, be a terrifying thought if God's were only a perfecting love, only a love committed to making us pure and spotless, and not also an accepting and forgiving love. But when God dwells in us, though we cannot help but tremble at the thought, he comes because he cares for us.

Jesus, thou art all compassion,
Pure, unbounded love thou art;
Visit us with thy salvation,
Enter ev'ry trembling heart.

In Jesus, God comes to bless. He brings the blessing of
the kingdom of heaven. That is the message of the opening
verses of Matthew 5, verses we have come to call the "Beatitudes." Everyone loves the Beatitudes — and, though we
might be hard pressed to explain a few of them if anyone
were to ask, somehow we find them comforting. They speak
to all sorts and conditions of people, who find in them the
simple message that, in Jesus, God comes to bless.

"Blessed," Jesus says. In the Latin translation Christians
used for centuries: *beatus,* from which we get the name Beatitudes. It really means something like, "Oh the blessedness
of. . . ." Oh the blessedness of those who are poor in spirit. Oh
the blessedness of those who mourn. Understanding the
blessings in that way we will not be tempted to read them as
conditions: blessed are you *if* you are poor in spirit; blessed
are you *if* you mourn; and so forth. That is not what Jesus
means.

Notice to whom he speaks here. "When he saw the
crowds, he went up on a mountainside and sat down. His disciples came to him, and he began to teach them." He speaks
not to just anyone but to his disciples. Those he has called.
Those whom his gracious hand has touched. And he paints
for them a picture of life under God's rule. It is not like the
greatness of any other kingdom. It is to be poor in spirit, to be
meek, to be a peacemaker. Not what the world counts as
greatness — or as blessedness. And yet, to the disciples he

64

has called to be with him, Jesus pictures this life as one of bliss. "Oh the blessedness of" this life to which he has called them; for it is a life that acknowledges God's rule.

So in these blessings Jesus sets down no conditions for entering the kingdom. He establishes no law for governing the world. But he places the name of God and the blessing of God upon his followers. For, ultimately, only God can bless, and it is his blessing alone that we need.

How shall we describe the substance of Jesus' blessings? Notice the structure of the Beatitudes: eight blessings, each with a promise attached. Usually the promise is in the future tense. But in the first and eighth the promise is present tense, and it is the same promise: "theirs is the kingdom of heaven." The divine love has come to earth and fixed in us his humble dwelling. And where that love dwells, there is God's rule, God's kingdom. This is what Jesus gives — eight descriptions of the life of the kingdom. Listen again to the first four.

> Oh the blessedness of the poor in spirit,
>   for theirs is the kingdom of heaven.
> Oh the blessedness of those who mourn,
>   for they will be comforted.
> Oh the blessedness of the meek,
>   for they will inherit the earth.
> Oh the blessedness of those who hunger and thirst
>   for righteousness,
>   for they will be filled.

We should not be too quick to spiritualize these beatitudes. Indeed, where Matthew's Gospel says "blessed are the poor in spirit," Luke's Gospel has simply, "blessed are you poor." When the psalmist says (in one of the verses Jesus must have in mind), "The Lord hears the needy," he means the poor, the oppressed, the persecuted. When the prophet announces the work which the Servant of God upon whom God's Spirit rests will do, he speaks of binding up the broken-hearted and freeing the prisoner. Of comforting those who mourn — not just over their sins, but those who mourn because of loss. And when the meek are promised that they will inherit the earth, Jesus is referring to the words of the psalmist: "the meek shall possess the land." What land? The promised land of milk and honey. And those who hunger and thirst for righteousness are, in the first sense, those beaten down by injustice, who cry to God for a king who will execute justice and righteousness in the land.

God cares about their cares. God cares about those who can find no justice in our world; about those whose backs are broken by poverty; about those who have suffered great loss and find little comfort; about those without home or homeland. How should God not care about them when God has himself been one of them? The foxes may have holes and the birds of the air nests, but when God lived among us he had nowhere to lay his head. He was pursued by hostile opponents. He belonged to an oppressed people, dominated by a foreign power. He was convicted and executed as a criminal. How should God not care about the poor, the mournful, the meek, the oppressed? And if God cares about all this, then to care about it is a blessing, to care about it is to live under God's rule. That much is sure.

But we should also not fail to spiritualize the beatitudes. Not all will be poor, but all must be poor in spirit, must look to God for every need. Not all will mourn great losses, but all must mourn their separation from the God whose presence is joy. Not all will be homeless, but all must seek the city whose Maker is God. Not all will go hungry and suffer great injustice, but all must hunger to be pronounced righteous by God.

And whatever our present lot may be, whatever it may become, the promise of these blessings is sure. For that one man who had nowhere to lay his head, who was abandoned by his dearest friends, who was convicted and executed — that man was not abandoned by the heavenly Father. He is the One who promises: those who mourn will be comforted with divine comfort; the meek will be given the land of promise; those who hunger to be set right with God will have that hunger filled. And to be poor in spirit, to know that every blessing comes from the hand of God — that simply *is* to live in the kingdom of heaven.

Four more descriptions of the kingdom:

Oh the blessedness of the merciful,
　　for they will be shown mercy.
Oh the blessedness of the pure in heart,
　　for they will see God.
Oh the blessedness of the peacemakers,
　　for they will be called sons of God.
Oh the blessedness of those who are persecuted
　　　because of righteousness,
　　for theirs is the kingdom of heaven.

If the first four beatitudes seem to concentrate upon this life — upon poverty, loss, homelessness, and injustice — the last four seem to press us ahead. Ahead to the end of the story, to the final coming of the kingdom in glory. The merciful will be shown mercy — definitively. The pure in heart will see God — upon whom no one can look in this life. The peacemakers will be called children of God — when the family of God is gathered.

Then the earth will have no choice but to receive her king. Fields, rocks, hills, and plains will sing with joy at their release from the bondage to which creation has been subjected. And the king will rule the world with truth and grace. Then we will see what for now we can only believe. How blessed then will be the merciful, for only they will not complain about the mercy God has shown others. How blessed will be the pure in heart, for only they will really want to see God as he is and not simply as they have imagined him to be. How blessed will be the peacemakers, for only they will delight in the company of all who are called children of God. How blessed will be those persecuted because of righteousness; only they will not be ashamed to bend the knee to a persecuted and crucified God.

And when we think of all the blessings Jesus speaks here — the blessedness of a humble spirit, the blessedness of seeking our comfort in God, of waiting for the land he has promised, of hungering to be filled with his true righteousness, the blessedness of showing mercy as he has shown it, of a heart so pure that it longs to be with God, of a heart so at peace with God that it can entrust itself to his keeping, of a heart so at one with God that it will gladly suffer for Christ's sake — when we think of this as a picture of life in God's kingdom, we see what a reversal it is of the standards by which our world judges happiness and by which all too often we judge it. For our world is not likely to say: "Oh the blessedness of one who goes to a cross because God wills it." Yet he is the One the Father raised; he is the blessed One in whom the world's verdict is reversed and the kingdom comes.

In blessing us, in making us citizens of that kingdom, Jesus commits himself to begin in us the same great reversal. The divine glory will shine in and through our lives. As the hymn says of God's children:

> They are lights upon the earth,
> Children of a heavenly birth;
> One with God, with Jesus won;
> Glory is in them *begun*.

That is the blessing. Glory, divine glory, in us begun. And in the great hymn with which we began Charles Wesley has given us the words with which to respond to this gift, to the beginning of glory in us.

> *Finish*, then, thy new creation;
> Pure and spotless let us be.
> Let us see thy great salvation
> Perfectly restored in thee.
> Changed from glory into glory,
> Till in heav'n we take our place,
> Till we cast our crowns before thee,
> Lost in wonder, love, and praise.

13. Children of the Light

*You are the light of the world. . . . Let your light shine be-
fore men, that they may see your good deeds and praise
your Father in heaven.*

MATTHEW 5:14, 16

*Jesus spoke to them saying, "I am the light of the world;
he who follows me will not walk in darkness, but will
have the light of life."*

JOHN 8:12

Last week we heard Jesus' word to his people in the Beatitudes. There he sets the name and the blessing of God upon
his followers. "Theirs is the kingdom of heaven." But there is
more to Matthew's fifth chapter than those blessings. Before
we've finished the chapter we will have to struggle with some
hard sayings.

Consider the two passages I have juxtaposed here. In

John 8 Jesus says, "I am the light of the world." In Matthew 5 he says to his followers, "You are the light of the world." The tension between those two verses is the tension of the Christian life. The light has shined into your life; now let your light shine. Jesus is the light; his light is to shine through our lives. We are evidently to be mirrors, obediently reflecting his goodness. His light shines through our lives when others see our good deeds and praise the Father in heaven.

It may be that Matthew intends to picture Jesus as a new Moses. There are in Matthew's Gospel five great discourses of Jesus, long sections containing Jesus' teaching — just as there are in the Old Testament the five books of Moses. And in the first of Matthew's five discourses, the Sermon on the Mount which begins with chapter five, Jesus quite clearly reinterprets the Decalog, the law Moses had received from the Lord.

Last week we emphasized the promise embedded in the blessings. Today we hear first the requirement discipleship brings. "Do not think that I have come to abolish the Law or the Prophets," Jesus says. "I have come not to abolish them but to fulfill them." Not even the tiniest of Hebrew letters nor even one of the small strokes making a little swirl on a letter may be omitted from the law "until everything is accomplished." Only those who both do and teach these commands will be called great in the kingdom.

In the history of Christian interpretation of the Bible these verses have caused more than a little bewilderment. They seem at first glance to demand a total acceptance of the Old Testament law — not only in its moral but also in its cultic and ceremonial requirements. Yet we know that the early Christians did not consider themselves thus bound to keep the law. The mission to the Gentiles made clear, for example, that circumcision was not necessary for the non-Jew who wanted to become a follower of Christ. Still more, we know that the very Jesus who speaks these words himself sometimes seems to act differently — when he defends his disciples for a seeming violation of sabbath law; or, even later in this fifth chapter of Matthew, in passages we will come to during the next two weeks, when he reinterprets the moral law given by Moses.

So this is a puzzle. Neither Jesus himself nor his first followers did precisely what these verses seem to require. Perhaps we need to look again — and think again — about Jesus' words here. Certainly he is telling his followers that obedience matters in discipleship, that God's will is to shine through their lives and enlighten the world. But Jesus is talking about more than rules here. He speaks not of the law simply but of "the Law and the Prophets" — a phrase describing the entire Old Testament. He has, he says, come to fulfill them. He has come to fulfill the law, to obey it. And not a jot or tittle of it will be forgotten until everything is accomplished, until he can say "it is finished." He has come to fulfill the prophets — to be the One they had promised.

But more than this, he has come to give both law and prophets their full meaning. He fulfills them when he unfolds for us that meaning. Only in him, the One who is the light of the world, do we see the full meaning of what the prophets longed for and promised. And only from him do we learn the full meaning of God's will for our lives — what it really means to be holy as the heavenly Father is holy. During the next two weeks we will let Jesus be the new Moses, showing us what holiness truly requires. Not only is killing forbidden, but even anger. Not only adultery, but even lust. He will unfold the full meaning of discipleship. We will learn from him what it means to let our light shine that others may see our good deeds and glorify the heavenly Father.

We must ask in all seriousness that Jesus unfold the full meaning of discipleship in us — in our lives. The Christ born as a small child is a God big enough for the world, and the glory has shone not just upon Israel but upon the Gentiles as well — upon all peoples. For all of them we are to be a light. Which also means of course: a light for those in our family, for the person next door, the person at work, the person in the desk beside us at school. If the glory of the kingdom, the light of Christ, is to shine into every nook and cranny of our world, it will have to shine into and through our lives. "You are the light of the world," Jesus says. "Let your light shine."

And yet, even this is not simply a requirement. Jesus does come to give the law its full meaning, to show us what the obedience of discipleship requires. But he comes to fulfill the Law *and* the Prophets — to give the full meaning to that deliverance of which the prophets spoke. He is, therefore, more than a new Moses. When Moses says to us: You shall have no other gods — you shall not covet — you shall honor your father and mother — you shall not steal . . . we may hear first the requirement: You shall. But when Jesus reinterprets the Decalog for us, when we hear from him "you shall," we hear more than a requirement. We hear also a promise. You shall have no other gods. That's the way you'll really be. You shall not covet. You shall honor your father and mother. You shall be perfect. That is a promise; for he has committed himself to the task of perfecting us.

You are the light of the world. Let your light shine. That

sounds like a requirement. And it is — one we do well to heed. But remember who speaks here, who requires this of us. The same One who says, "I am the light of the world; he who follows me will not walk in darkness, but will have the light of life." The disciple will have the light of life. That is a promise.

The requirements of discipleship are many, and they can be hard. But they carry no threat; for in them we hear the promise of the One who is the light of the world, the One who has shined into the darkness of our hearts, the One who will make us — fully and completely — children of the light. And the praise, then, will belong entirely to him — and to his Father, to whom he himself directs our praise. "Let your light shine before men, that they may see your good deeds and praise your Father in heaven."

14. The Perfection of Love

For I tell you, that unless your righteousness surpasses
that of the Pharisees and the teachers of the law, you will
certainly not enter the kingdom of heaven.

MATTHEW 5:20

If we give ourselves to the One who is love, the One who made us in his image and sought us when we turned from him, what will he ask of us? The answer to that question is given in Matthew 5, where Jesus outlines the new righteousness of the kingdom. Today and next week we will hear Jesus deepen, strengthen, and reinterpret the Decalog until he brings his description of the righteousness of the kingdom to its climax at the end of the chapter by saying: "You, therefore, must be perfect, as your heavenly Father is perfect."

That is what he has in mind. Perhaps, though, perfection — and, at that, a perfection like unto God's — sounds a bit too much to ask. Perhaps we need to start with a more human standard. And Jesus himself does that. "Unless your righteousness surpasses that of the Pharisees and the teachers of the law, you will certainly not enter the kingdom of heaven." That sounds a little more doable. Who were these folk we are to surpass — the scribes, and the Pharisees? The scribes, the teachers of the law, were just that: students of the Torah, the Old Testament law. They were the professional theologians of their day, who had dedicated their entire lives to the study and teaching of the Scriptures.

The Pharisees? Well, remember the little parable Jesus once told, comparing a Pharisee and a Publican. You recall that it was the Publican, the tax collector, who simply said, "God be merciful to me, a sinner," and who, according to Jesus, went down to his house justified. But what of the Pharisee? His problem, of course we remember, was his self-righteousness. But what sort of man was he? We can recall the credentials he lists, credentials we have no reason to doubt. He points out that he was not an unjust man; he was not an illegal extortioner, as that Publican surely was; nor was he an adulterer. On the positive side, he fasted twice a week; he gave a tithe of all he possessed.

Not bad. And that was typical of the Pharisees. They were not bad at all. In fact, they were among the most pious of Jews. Good, solid, religious-minded folk. More than that — they were serious believers who knew that the religious life of their people was in need of considerable renewal. And Jesus says to us: "Unless your righteousness surpasses that of the Pharisees and the teachers of the law, you will certainly not enter the kingdom of heaven." Perhaps we now pause. Those Pharisees are no easy mark. They set a rather lofty standard. What can Jesus have in mind?

When today and next week Jesus unfolds the full meaning of the law, he does so in a way that emphasizes especially two general themes:

- He makes clear that the law applies not just to external acts, but even to wishes, desires, emotions, and feelings. Not only is killing wrong; even anger with the brother is forbidden. Not just adultery, but also lust is forbidden. Hatred for the enemy or a desire for vengeance — even those quite natural feelings are ruled out. That is the first way in which Jesus unfolds the full meaning of the law.
- He teaches that his disciples are to make themselves vulnerable — by not retaliating when evil is done us, by not demanding reciprocity from those we help, by trusting the word of another without any demand that he give more than his word.

In these two ways Jesus unfolds in the Sermon on the Mount the full meaning of the law. It speaks not just of the deed but of the inner person, and it requires vulnerability before others. This is the righteousness of the kingdom, the righteousness that surpasses that of the scribes and Pharisees. We will leave for next week the second of these emphases — the requirement of vulnerability. For today it will be enough to take note of the way Jesus extends the laws even to thoughts, desires, and emotions. Our reaction to his doing so is likely to be, first, that we don't much care for it, and, second, that it doesn't make much sense.

We don't really care for this way of unfolding the full meaning of the law, this notion that the law somehow applies to the whole person, not just to the deed. We rather like to be able to say exactly and precisely what we did wrong. That way there's always a chance we can correct it and balance the slate. But the standard Jesus sets here doesn't seem to allow that. It doesn't allow for just a correction here or there, a change of heart now and then, a minor adjustment or two in what we do, an attempt to be a little better tomorrow than we were today. That we might manage with some success. But Jesus' standard seems to call for a complete transformation of character — that we become new people. And that's more than we can manage. We didn't create ourselves to begin with. We're not likely to manage to re-create ourselves.

So we may not care much for the way Jesus extends the meaning of the law here. Still more, we may wonder whether it really makes sense. It makes sense to command me to do something that is within my power, to command me to act or not to act in certain ways. But what sense does it make to command me not to have certain desires or feelings? They just spring up unbidden within me. No one can control them. Trying to make a law for them seems useless.

And that's the point, isn't it? Sunday after Sunday we confess our sin. But this is what it means: that we're torn and divided within ourselves. That even when we do the good, we may often do it in the face of contrary desires. That even when we manage to stifle the angry feeling or the vengeful word, it's still there stifled within us — part of us. The righteousness of the kingdom which Jesus depicts here asks of us more than a little progress or a few adjustments. Jesus is saying neither more nor less than he once said to Nicodemus in a conversation recounted in John's Gospel: You must be born again. You must become a new person. You must hand yourself over to God and ask him to pardon what is amiss and to empower you to live a new life.

If it were just a matter of external deeds, those Pharisees would be hard men to beat. But it's not just that. It's a new creation Jesus has in mind. And for that we need once more the presence of the Creator. One with the authority to say: You have heard it said, but I say to you. One who does more than require that we let our light shine; One who is the light of the world, shining into our darkness. To him we turn in repentance and trust, and give ourselves to him even as he seeks us.

The Jesus who here unfolds the full meaning of the law for us, the perfection of love and the wholeness of heart and mind which the law requires, will not be ashamed to own us as his people when we confess that this is a perfection beyond our power to create in our lives. For he is the One who has said to us, "Blessed are the poor in spirit; theirs is the kingdom of heaven." The Jesus who here asks more of us than we can naturally manage is the crucified and risen One who promises to send into our hearts his own Spirit of new life and power. This is the Jesus who has said to us, "Blessed are those who hunger and thirst for righteousness, for they shall be filled."

The perfection of love he requires is the perfection of love he both enacts and gives. And in response to him, to his gift of righteousness and his call to righteousness, we can and should say in the words of Charles Wesley's great hymn: "O Love, I give myself to thee, thine ever, only thine, to be."

15. Vulnerable Love

You have heard that it was said, "Eye for eye, and tooth for tooth." But I tell you, Do not resist an evil person. If someone strikes you on the right cheek, turn to him the other also.

MATTHEW 5:38-39

For four weeks now we have heard the words of Christ in Matthew's fifth chapter. We have heard the blessings of Christ upon his people . . . the command to be a light in our world, empowered by Christ's own light in our life . . . the requirement of a new righteousness that reorders our entire life and calls upon us to become new people. And now today — in what may seem to be the most demanding of all Jesus' hard sayings — he spells out for us the meaning of love: Turning the other cheek. Giving freely to those who only wanted to borrow from us. Loving the enemy. Not resisting one who is evil. In short — to love as he would have us love is to be vulnerable.

These are, I said, often called "hard sayings." But what makes them hard? Are they hard simply because they require a kind of love almost impossible to achieve in human life? We might think that — and surely some have understood the hard sayings in that way. They have heard in them a demand for a non-retaliatory pacifism which would be hard indeed — and possibly wrong — for any society to practice. How shall the weak be cared for if none will defend them? How shall justice be done if no one will fight for it? How do we guard against cheaters and slackers if anyone in need is just given whatever he wants? Sometimes we have questions like those in mind when we think of these sayings as hard. They're hard because no society could really practice them, because they state an ideal impossible for us to live out in our world. Maybe, we might be tempted to think, Jesus wasn't really serious.

But he was — and so we need to ask what he means here, what sort of righteousness it is which exceeds that of the scribes and Pharisees. In our world today many people are more and more reluctant to support the use of military force; yet, almost everyone accepts as a matter of course that we have a right to defend ourselves, to press our own rights, our claims, our entitlements.

The righteousness of the kingdom that Jesus here sets forth is exactly the opposite: He does not require that we never use force, if force is necessary to defend neighbors in need or innocent victims. He does not require that we renounce entirely an economic system based on lending and borrowing, if it truly serves the needs of many neighbors. He does not say, if someone strikes your neighbor on his right cheek, turn that neighbor's other cheek to be struck as well.

Jesus does not here legislate for society. He speaks to his people, to us, and tells us not to defend ourselves, not to pour energy into making certain everyone respects our rights. Not to do this — *so that* the very same energy can be used to defend the rights of our neighbors.

Our world says: Look out for yourself — don't risk defending others. Jesus says that the righteousness of the kingdom is the opposite: Make yourself vulnerable — for the sake of others. That is indeed a hard saying. Not hard because it requires Christians to renounce force used in behalf of others. About that Jesus says nothing. But hard because it requires us not to defend ourselves — to be vulnerable.

That is, to be sure, hard — hard to hear, hard to live. But we have still not gotten to what really makes it hard. It is hard precisely because Jesus is so serious — so serious that he not only asks that we make ourselves vulnerable but reveals to us a vulnerable God. A God who suffers, who accepts insults done him without retaliating in kind, a God who forgives those driving nails into his hands and feet. Can we really admire or love a God like that? Of course we say we do, but we don't want to be vulnerable ourselves. We don't really admire vulnerability. We're not often attracted to people who don't stand up for their rights.

There's a story by Richard Jefferies about a little boy reading a picture book which tells the story of the crucifixion. He stares a long time at the picture of Jesus on the cross, finally turns the page, and says: "If God had been there, he would not have let it happen."

That little boy speaks for us, at least in some of our moods. He — and we — don't always want that tender Jesus, meek and mild. It can be hard to believe that it's God on the cross, willingly there to suffer. We might prefer a strong God who won't let people take advantage of him, who won't let anyone get from him something they don't have coming. We're a little like that older brother in the parable of the Prodigal Son. He expressed anger that his father should receive the younger brother back. But we sense more than anger there — also scorn. Scorn for a father silly enough to be duped by a son who took what he could get and now comes running back only because he's in need. Scorn for a father who'll let that son get what he has no claim to. And we know instinctively what Jesus leaves unsaid, what lies in the future for this father and his older son. Anger and scorn will erupt into hostility — and the father's love, this time for the older son, will once more make him vulnerable. We have a lot in common with that older brother.

Do we really want or admire a God like that father — one that vulnerable? Well, there's at least one case in which we do. Our own. I may think God ought to give you what you have coming, but I don't really want him to treat me that way. I may think that only a crazy father would love someone who seems almost worthless, but that's the sort of father I want when I'm the prodigal. Whatever standards I may think he should apply to the rest of you, I don't want him to receive me only when I deserve it. For you, perhaps — sternness. For me — meek and mild. When it comes to that, to our own skin, we want the father who'll come running out, happy to receive us back. We're all glad to sing for ourselves, "My hope is built on nothing less than Jesus' blood and righteousness."

The God Jesus reveals to us is a vulnerable God — One willing to take his chances with us, willing to be vulnerable before us. Not too proud to take whatever we dish out and still receive us when we turn back. That God, who makes himself vulnerable before us, calls us now to be vulnerable before others. Not to sing, "My hope is built on nothing less than Jesus' blood and righteousness," without also learning to sing, "Jesus, I my cross have taken, all to leave and follow thee."

"Be perfect," Jesus says, "as your heavenly Father is perfect." Which must mean: be vulnerable, as your heavenly Father is vulnerable. As we want him to be vulnerable for us. As he has been vulnerable before us when we crucified him.

That vulnerability is the deepest mystery of the divine glory we have traced throughout this fifth chapter of Matthew. The One who calls upon us to be lights in the world is himself the light shining into our lives. The One who depicts the strict righteousness of the kingdom, a righteousness that calls for an inner transformation of our person, is himself the re-creator and renewer. And the One who says, "in love be vulnerable," has himself carried the cross. This is the glory of Christ, the glory that shines into our world. The glory of One born vulnerable for our sakes. One fit to receive the worship of the Magi — but forced to flee the wrath of a king. He can be trusted when he says: Blessed are the meek, for they shall inherit the earth. Blessed are the peacemakers, for they shall be called children of God. Blessed are the merciful, for they shall obtain mercy.

IV. Love Taking Shape in Time

To talk simply of "love," or even of "life in the kingdom," has about it a certain generality that may sometimes not seem to capture the thickness — the "locatedness" — of our lives. One way to gain specificity we have already explored — using the commands of the Decalog to reflect upon particular bonds of life. Another way is to pay attention to the moments that punctuate our life: birth, marriage, death. Or the places that mark us, such as the country in which we live and to which we are loyal. Or the commonplace and everyday — working and sleeping. Thus, our attempt to live in love takes account of our limits, our finitude, as it takes shape in time and place. Our love becomes, as the seventeenth-century Anglican bishop, Jeremy Taylor, put it, "fitted for society."

We may pray for all and wish well to all (though, if we are honest, this is hard enough), but we must live and work in particular places with particular people. We will be attached to them in special ways, and they may mourn our death in ways that others do not. To say anything less than this would be to think of ourselves as free-floating, rather than embodied, spirits. The sermons that follow take account of just some of these particular locations which mark the identity of finite human beings.

In the funeral homily, "The End of the Day," I have fictionalized the name of the deceased, since I could not, of course, ask her permission to speak of her life and death. "Fellow Fetuses" is specific to the season of Epiphany, that season of the liturgical year in which the church marvels that divine glory should be shown in the person and life of the child born of Mary. Because the Supreme Court's *Roe v. Wade* decision was first handed down in January of 1973, the Epiphany season provides an apt moment to reflect upon love for the unborn. "Fellow Fetuses" was first published in *Lutheran Forum* (Christmas, 1998). If "Love Abides," the homily for a marriage, seems a bit more personal than one might ordinarily expect, that is because it was preached at the wedding of one of my daughters. It was first published in the *Christian Century* (October 11, 2000). In addition to the obvious debts that are acknowledged along the way, I am conscious that "To Love One's Homeland" bears the mark of C. S. Lewis's influence — both his *Reflections on the Psalms* and his *The Four Loves.*

16. Fellow Fetuses

Speak yourself on behalf of the dumb,
*   on behalf of all the unwanted;*
speak yourself, pronounce a just verdict,
*   and uphold the rights of the poor, of the needy.*

PROVERBS 31:8-9

It was on January 22, 1973, that the Supreme Court of our country, in the *Roe v. Wade* decision, gave legal sanction to a permissive abortion policy. The toll of abortions in this country since that January day more than a quarter century ago reaches well into the millions — reason enough for Christians to be concerned. There are, to be sure, many others besides the unborn who are in need of our concern, but we are not wrong today to permit the words of the Israelite sage to invite us to think together about abortion.

The Epiphany glory of the child — the child! — in the manger shines into our world through the words and deeds of those who have come to kneel and worship. And through us when we open our mouths and speak on behalf of those who are unwanted and unable to speak for themselves. In their time of need, the Body of Christ must be the epiphany of God in our world.

Still, some things should be preached and others taught. A sermon is not the place to sort through every difficult case that comes along, nor is it the place to resolve the complexities of moral decision-making. But a sermon *is* the place to consider what it means that we should be the epiphany of God in a culture for which abortion has become everyday and commonplace.

We should, first, understand a little of what is at stake. The abortion controversy in this country will not go away one day soon. There will continue to be conflict — and, even, violence. For at no time in our history since the Civil War have we confronted an issue in which the very definition of ourselves as a people has been so directly involved. We are arguing about whose good counts in the common good we share. Does the fetus also count? How inclusive — or how narrow — are the boundaries of the human community among us?

To understand that this is the question is to realize that we Christians are not without insight. Perhaps the simplest and most striking way to state our insight is to say, as Paul Ramsey once did: We are — all of us — fellow fetuses. All without the ability to speak for ourselves in the court that really counts — before God. All in need of a Vindicator to speak on our behalf. All without claims or achievements that count for anything in that divine court — and eagerly seeking a Defender who will, on our behalf, uphold the poor and needy.

When we think of the central themes of the Bible, we do

not usually start with the Book of Proverbs. Yet, if the Bible has any central theme at all, it is one not far removed from the passage with which we began. God is a God who acts to deliver those who cannot save themselves. This God — who set his hand upon Israel, upon Mary, and upon the child born to her — is no respecter of persons. Strong or weak, valued or unwanted, it makes little difference to this God.

If we seek to be the epiphany of God in our world, we must be radically ill at ease when worth is measured in terms of achievement, or mental capacity, or power, or whether someone else wants us. To know ourselves as fellow fetuses must mean that we will be very reluctant indeed to narrow the bounds of the human community among us. That is the first insight Christian vision offers.

But there is also a second truth that we should see. Moved by our hope and trust in God, determined to be his epiphany in the world, we must seek to become people who are eager to receive children into the human family. We do not want to find ourselves on Herod's side. Madeleine L'Engle has powerfully expressed this truth in her poem, "The Risk of Birth."

> This is no time for a child to be born
> With the earth betrayed by war & hate
> And a nova lighting the sky to warn
> That time runs out & the sun burns late.
>
> That was not time for a child to be born,
> In a land in the crushing grip of Rome;
> Honour & truth were trampled by scorn —
> Yet here did the Saviour make his home.

When is the time for love to be born?
The inn is full on the planet earth,
And by greed & pride the sky is torn —
Yet Love still takes the risk of birth.

G. K. Chesterton once pointed out that we should not underestimate the power of the Christmas story to shape Christian life and thought. Those pictures we have seen since we were young children . . . those stories we have heard time and again . . . all ringing the changes on that single mysterious theme: "that the hands that made the sun and stars were too small to reach the huge heads of the cattle." The hands of God were poor and needy when given into the care of Mary and Joseph; they are poor and needy still when given into our care.

The divine blessing spoken at the creation — "be fruitful and multiply" — continues to be effective in our world. And the presence of children is a sign of God's continuing "yes" to his creation, testimony that he will not withdraw from the time and history in which he has become incarnate. We welcome children into our midst therefore and speak on behalf of the unwanted not because we can protect them from all the dangers of life, not because they are such lovable little things, not because their potential is great — but in order to be in this world the epiphany of the God who came to us as Mary's child.

Such an attitude may not seem rational to all our neighbors, but it reflects the deeper mystery of God's own reason. For, as Madeleine L'Engle put it in another of her poems of the incarnation:

This is the irrational season
When love blooms bright and wild.
Had Mary been filled with reason
There'd have been no room for the child.

And, hence, whatever the complexities of moral decision-making, whatever our hopes and fears in a troubled world, whatever reasons our too-fearful reason may put forward, we fellow fetuses — Christ's Body in our world — should not forget that "Love still takes the risk of birth." Love bestows worth upon the weak and unwanted; love speaks on behalf of the child in need. And we should not grow so old that we forget what it was like to be a child and to sing at Christmas: "Bless all the dear children in thy tender care."

17. Love Abides

"Love never ends," St. Paul writes in the lesson we read from 1 Corinthians 13. Or, put more positively, "love abides." What does that really mean — to say that "love abides"? Or, indeed, what possible sense could it make to say this in a world in which the truth so clearly seems to be that love quite often does not abide?

We pause for a moment in this service in order to think about just that question. And we do this not primarily for the sake of Hannah and Christopher. No, we do it for our own sake, because the church needs regularly to remind itself what marriage actually means. We do it so that together we can think about how it might be that Hannah and Chris, or any of the rest of us, might solemnly vow "not to part till death parts us."

It's a crazy thing to do, really. That two relatively young people should together reach out and take hold of their future in this way — should determine that, come what may, it will be a future together — that can hardly make sense. Unless, perhaps, God makes sense of it for us. For the miracle and the mystery of marriage is that God permits us to exercise just a little of his own creative power — to determine this one thing about our future: that it will be a future together. And having permitted us to be as creative as he himself is, God then asks us — and invites us — to learn also to be as steadfast and faithful as he is.

What might God hope to accomplish through such a crazy invitation? God has in mind to get something done in us and to us. Stanley Hauerwas, who teaches theology and ethics at Duke Divinity School, and who almost never fails to be provocative, once wrote that the most basic law of marriage could be stated in a sentence. "You always marry the wrong person." This is what he wrote: "You always marry the wrong person. The one thought to be Mr. Right turns out not to be. Ms. Right tends to show up after marriage. But the adventure of marriage is learning to love the person to whom you are married. . . . Love does not create a marriage; marriage teaches us what a costly adventure love is."

He's deliberately made the point a little provocatively, but it is nonetheless true. Of course, for anyone who is married, it is true that you may not be married now to the person you once thought you were marrying. Five years from now, or ten years from now, the person sitting next to you won't necessarily be the person you thought you were giving yourself to. So if marriage requires us to choose just exactly the right person . . . well, we're in very big trouble. The target keeps shifting. Marrying means promising to be faithful to someone who may keep changing. And so, the church does not ask today, "Christopher, *do* you love Hannah?" but rather, "Christopher, *will* you love Hannah?" "Hannah, *will* you love Christopher?"

Marriage, therefore, does not exist primarily to make us happy but to make us holy — though in the long run, of course, there can be no happiness apart from holiness. But it's holiness that God is after. And so, in marriage God goes to work on us — begins to teach us what it means, what it will require of us, to love even just this one person as God loves each of us, with steadfastness and faithfulness. Every marriage will be different, of course, and so the lesson will have to come in different ways, but it has a chance to happen for us only as we accept the discipline of marriage as God's good gift to us.

So, for example, Chris — a young man who is, if I may say so, almost obsessively neat — is going to have to learn to love Hannah, who is her mother's daughter, and who therefore never met a scrap of paper or a piece of junk that she didn't think should be saved somewhere. And Hannah, who has grown up in a household in which cars are things that are washed once or, at the very most, perhaps twice a year, things in which you eat hamburgers, french fries, candy, and ice cream — Hannah is going to have to learn to love someone who is deeply devoted to a spotless and shiny car. This will not always be easy. Chris, a fairly reserved and quiet fellow, is going to have to learn what it means to be talked to all the time. And Hannah is somehow going to have to learn that, as Kierkegaard says, "silence also belongs to conversation at times."

They will have to learn these things, and have opportunity to learn them, precisely because, by God's grace, "love abides." God gives us time. That comes first — the time, the abiding, the commitment to abide in a love like God's, the love that joins Father, Son, and Spirit. And when that comes first, when — as God's gift — you have a duty to abide, when you know that this other person is not just someone you fell in love with but (to paraphrase Will Willimon) "the one you're stuck with," then very gradually we may learn. Then God slowly begins to make of us the people he wants us to be, draws us into his own love — the only sort of love that truly abides.

In his book titled *Works of Love,* Søren Kierkegaard, that tormented genius of nineteenth-century Denmark, wrote a series of chapters reflecting upon the themes of 1 Corinthians 13. One of his chapters is titled simply "Love Abides," and in that chapter are two of the most unforgettable and powerful pages that I have ever read. I was tempted just to read them to you today, but I didn't think that would work too well. So, instead, I will try simply to capture their flavor for a moment — if only in summary form.

Kierkegaard pictures two people (lover-beloved, joined by the hyphen that is God's own love, the love which abides), but two people who no longer seem able to sustain their bond. "And so the breaking-point between the two is reached," he writes. The beloved turns away. But, says Kierkegaard, the lover keeps the hyphen: "lover-." Imagine, Kierkegaard says, that you saw nothing but a word followed by a hyphen. What would you say? You would say that the word is not yet complete. Consequently, the lover — who wills to abide in the eternal love that is God's — believes that the relationship which another considers broken is a relationship that has not yet been completed. The lover abides.

Then Kierkegaard does it again, shifting the metaphor. "And so it came to the breaking-point." But the lover abides. He — or she — says: We're only halfway through this sentence, a sentence that is not yet complete. What a difference there is, Kierkegaard notes, between a sentence fragment and an unfinished sentence. And for the lover, who wills to abide, it cannot be a broken fragment. The sentence is simply not yet complete.

Then Kierkegaard does it yet again. "And so it came to the breaking-point." Lover and beloved are no longer speaking to each other. But, Kierkegaard writes, "the lover says: 'I abide; therefore we shall still speak with one another, because silence also belongs to conversation at times.'"

And once more Kierkegaard does it in one grand image, which I will, in fact, simply read to you: "Does the dance cease because one dancer has gone away? In a certain sense. But if the other still remains standing in the posture which expresses a turning towards the one who is not seen, and if [because you abide] you know nothing about the past, then you will say, 'Now the dance will begin just as soon as the other comes, the one who is expected.'"

Every time I read that, I try to picture it. The lover, standing there in the posture of the dancer, waiting for the beloved. Not assuming that the dance has ceased — but abiding. Expecting the beloved to come and the dance to begin again. I try to picture it.

It seems like a rather awkward posture, doesn't it? One could get a cramp — or lots of cramps. A stiff neck. One could tire. One could become impatient. But that is why God gives us time, gives us marriage: that we may not tire, but, on the contrary, gain joy in abiding. And that, Hannah and Chris, is why God gives you time, gives you marriage today — that slowly and patiently you may be drawn into God's own love, a love stronger and more steadfast than comes naturally to you or to any of us. That you may be drawn into the dance of love that never ends, because, as St. Paul says, "love never ends." Love abides.

18. Lives of Praise

I appeal to you, therefore, brethren, by the mercies of God, to present your bodies as a living sacrifice, holy and acceptable to God, which is your spiritual worship.

ROMANS 12:1

"That in these gray and latter days/There may be men whose life is praise," Martin Franzmann's great hymn says. But how easily we forget it. Forget that the gospel means freedom from the tyranny of good works — so that we may serve God in the whole of our life with good work. Work which in its quality and character would be an offering of praise and thanksgiving to God and would, therefore, serve our neighbors.

In its simplest and least complicated sense the word of the gospel announces that God is pleased with us, that God is on our side. Hence, anxiety about our fate, anxiety that might cripple our spirit and distort our work is dispelled. The energy that might have gone into trying to be sure that God is pleased with us is released for service to others. Freed from incessant introspection about our own fate, we may for the first time see rightly, see the tasks that God sets before us. Now we can do more than talk about freedom from sin and guilt; we can live as people who are really free.

Dorothy Sayers made the point well when she wrote: "The Church's approach to an intelligent carpenter is usually confined to exhorting him not to be drunk and disorderly in his leisure hours and to come to church on Sundays. What the Church *should* be telling him is this: that the very first demand that his religion makes upon him is that he should make good tables." Good work, honorable work of any kind offered to God, becomes one of the ways through which love takes shape in our lives.

When we allow ourselves to forget this, it is actually the neighbor in need of service whom we have forgotten. Our work is meant to serve not our own fulfillment, but that neighbor. That is its point, the reason for the tasks God sets before us. And to give that work anything less than our best is to miss the call of God and to shortchange the neighbor whom God wants to care for through us.

Christians have never been quite certain how best to make this point. On the one hand, it seems wrong to pretend that the work to which God calls us will always be satisfying, as if good work that needs doing were never laborious or tedious. Saying that God frees us for this work or calls us to it does not automatically turn work into play or into creative expression of our inner self. John Calvin, the great Reformer, made the point very directly: "Each man will bear and swallow the discomforts, vexations, weariness, and anxieties in his way of life, when he has been persuaded that the burden was laid upon him by God. From this will arise also a singular consolation: that no task will be so sordid and base, provided you obey your calling in it, that it will not shine and be reckoned very precious in God's sight." That gets it about right, doesn't it? The call of God does not magically erase the discomfort, vexation, weariness, and anxiety of our work. But it gives "consolation," the consolation of knowing that this work is precious to God because the worker is precious in his sight. Perhaps, indeed, we need a word that even goes beyond "consolation," a word such as "joy." Charles Wesley captured that joy in work God gives us in one of his hymns:

> Forth in thy name, O Lord, I go,
>   My daily labor to pursue,
> Thee, only thee resolved to know
>   In all I think, or speak, or do.
>
> The task thy wisdom has assigned
>   Oh, let me cheerfully fulfill,
> In all my works thy presence find,
>   And prove thy acceptable will.

"I appeal to you," St. Paul writes in Romans 12, "to present your bodies as a living sacrifice, holy and acceptable to God, which is your spiritual worship." Offer your *bodies*, Paul says. By which he makes clear that our response to God's grace is not some purely spiritual, ethereal response. It is bodily. Right here, in the material world of things, possessions, and jobs, the love God asks of us and elicits from us takes shape. Right here we find the neighbors whom God would have our work serve.

Offer your bodies a *living* sacrifice, Paul says — reminding us of the passage from the prophet Habakkuk which, in a sense, provides the theme of the entire Letter to the Romans. "He who through faith is righteous shall live." Faith brings God's acceptance and our security, not that we may simply bask in it but that we may *live*. That there may be those whose lives are praise. All those ordinary, garden-variety tasks that we carry out in our daily work — from reading books to stapling papers, from cooking meals to wiping runny noses, from repairing equipment to cutting hair to fixing teeth to managing an office — all that must become part of the worship we offer to God. A life of praise.

The just really do *live* by faith, for they are baptized into a Lord who lives, whom even death could not hold. The energy we might be tempted to expend seeking to secure our own lives can now be channeled into the work God gives us to do for others. And we can seek to do good work — not so that we can be accepted by God or by anyone else, but because we have been accepted in the only court of opinion that counts. Whether that work always brings joy, or even consolation, may be hard to say. Sometimes it may seem to be mostly discomfort, vexation, weariness, and anxiety. No matter. It is still true, as Einar Billing, a Scandanavian theologian, once wrote, that "joy over the forgiveness of sins is the only joy we should seek." And it is true, as Billing also put it, that our "one great discipline must be to attain to a new assurance of the forgiveness of sins through daily repentance and faith."

It is that simple, that straightforward, that life-transforming. The One whose presence you desire above all else, the Father who sent his Son to be with us and for us, is pleased with you. In repentance and faith, therefore, with the praise of God on our lips, we can go forth to pursue our daily labor. There to find the neighbor. There to carry out our spiritual worship. There to do, as best we can, good work. "That in these gray and latter days/There may be men whose life is praise."

19. To Love One's Homeland

By the waters of Babylon
we sat down and wept,
  when we remembered you, O Zion.
As for our harps, we hung them up
  on the trees in the midst of that land.
For those who led us away captive
asked us for a song,
and our oppressors called for mirth:
  "Sing us one of the songs of Zion."
How shall we sing the LORD's song
  in a strange land?
If I forget you, O Jerusalem,
  let my right hand forget its skill.
Let my tongue cleave to the roof of my mouth
if I do not remember you,
  if I do not set Jerusalem
  above my highest joy.
Remember the day of Jerusalem, O LORD,
against the people of Edom,

> *who said, "Down with it!*
> *down with it! even to the ground!"*
> *O daughter of Babylon,*
> *doomed to destruction,*
> > *happy the one who pays you back*
> > *for what you have done to us!*
> *Happy shall he be*
> *who takes your little ones*
> > *and dashes them against the rock!*

PSALM 137

That psalm is surely one of the most moving, and also one of the most troubling, in the entire Psalter. And it has much to teach Christians about what it means to have a homeland and to love one's country.

Recall your Old Testament history for a moment. After Solomon's reign the kingdom of Israel had been divided into a northern kingdom of Israel and a southern kingdom of Judah (with its capital at Jerusalem). The northern kingdom was annihilated by the Assyrians. A century-and-a-half later the kingdom of Judah was overrun by the Babylonians, and many of its inhabitants carried into exile. Finally, after a period of captivity, some of those exiles returned to Judah and rebuilt the walls of Jerusalem and the temple.

This psalm belongs to the last part of that history — written, probably, soon after the exiles had returned to Jerusalem and while the memory of captivity in Babylon remained fresh in their minds. The writer, who surely does not speak only for himself, remembers what it was like to be in a strange land, on alien soil.

By the waters of Babylon
we sat down and wept,
   when we remembered you, O Zion.

We can understand that he might weep. Not because Babylon was such a terrible place, not even simply because he was a captive, but because he was not at home — not in Zion, Jerusalem. Gone were the familiar sights, sounds, and places — the landmarks of life.

And so, he says, we hung up our harps. Our captors, mocking us a little, called for songs. They wanted to hear us sing the songs of Zion, our lost land. But, he writes, in perhaps the most famous line of the psalm,

How shall we sing the LORD's song
   in a strange land?

And the psalmist recalls how they had taken an oath not to forget their homeland.

Let my tongue cleave to the roof of my mouth
if I do not remember you,
   if I do not set Jerusalem
   above my highest joy.

At this point we're surely still with the writer. We still understand this most intense of human emotions: a love of home. And up to this point we have little trouble making his psalm our own song, our own prayer.

But then suddenly the mood shifts — as it does, in fact, in many psalms, but nowhere more violently than in Psalm

137. First the psalmist remembers the Edomites, ancient and bitter enemies of Israel. He recalls their reaction when Judah had been overrun by the powerful armies of Babylon — how the Edomites had urged the Babylonians on, calling upon them to destroy Jerusalem. How they had said,

> Down with it!
> down with it! even to the ground!

The psalmist has not forgotten, and he calls upon the Lord to remember and charge it to the account of the Edomites.

And then, in a rising crescendo of emotion which he can neither master nor control, the psalmist remembers the oppressor. He thinks of Babylon, and of the devastation Babylon had brought to Jerusalem. He calls upon Israel's God to remember to avenge Jerusalem.

> O daughter of Babylon,
> doomed to destruction,
>> happy the one who pays you back
>> for what you have done to us!
> Happy shall he be
> who takes your little ones
>> and dashes them against the rock!

He asks for nothing less than the utter destruction of Babylon. It was not unheard of among the nations of the time to dash babies upon the rocks. It was a way of killing the young and, thus, effectively exterminating a people. That is what the psalmist hopes and desires for the oppressor Babylon.

Happy shall he be
who takes your little ones
　　and dashes them against the rock!

And now, how shall we make this psalm our song, our
prayer? How include it in our worship?

We must, first, believe that the psalmist meant what he
said, that he hoped for the utter devastation of Babylon. But
he also meant what he says earlier in the psalm, when he de-
scribes the experience of every person who loves his place of
birth or his homeland. In the midst of all the splendor of Babylon, by the waters of Babylon — the Tigris and Euphrates,
and all the irrigation canals running off from them — there
he sat down and wept. On alien soil, in a strange land, he
could not sing.

That we can understand. Think of the town where you
grew up as a child. Perhaps it was nothing special. Perhaps,
even, to your adult eye it is now unattractive. Perhaps for
many people the sooner it is left behind, the better. But still
to you — is it not, also, home? There may be nothing in particular to recommend it. Certainly there are probably more
beautiful, more cultured, more satisfying places to live. Yet,
no one loves his home because it is better than all other
places. We love it simply because it is home — the place
where we are located, where our life has taken and been given
its characteristic shape.

This is as it should be. We are not gods — or even angels.
We are not free spirits. We are not even citizens of the world.
We are finite human beings, flesh and blood from the dust of
the ground — and we belong not everywhere, but somewhere
in particular. We can love our homeland not because it is

better than others but simply because it is ours, the one given us by the Creator, who sets the solitary in families. Even so that Israelite — carried off forcibly from Jerusalem to Babylon so many years ago — quite rightly took an oath always to remember Jerusalem. He was only doing what comes naturally to human beings: loving the land that was.

We can, then, make this psalm our own prayer when we acknowledge the true patriotism which moves the psalmist, and which should move us. But we must also see how easily this quite proper love of one's homeland can spill over into something terrible to behold. How quickly the psalmist moves from the plaintive cry that he cannot sing the Lord's song in a strange land to a cry for vengeance and destruction. How shall we pray that with him?

Perhaps we can pray it safely only as we imagine ourselves to be the Babylonians. Only as we think of ourselves as the oppressors who have brought this man to the point where he wishes what no human being ought ever desire. For we do not join him in his hatred when we say that we can understand it — that we can see how the agony and violence he and his fellow Israelites suffered at the hand of the Babylonians might have driven him to this point.

And, after all, there is something to his claim. He asks for vengeance, yes — and that we ought not ask for. But he asks also for just retribution. What a terrible thing it might be in the day of judgment to be a Babylonian who deserved — really deserved — such retribution. We can make this psalm our prayer as if we were that Babylonian. Remembering how easily we might become the oppressor. How, without thinking about it at all, we might lead someone to hate us as this Israelite hated Babylon. That much we can safely do — and should do.

Finally, when we make this psalm our prayer, we should remember that we cannot pray quite as that Israelite did. For we know, as he did not, that when God lived among us and loved his native land enough to weep over Jerusalem, it was nonetheless the powers of his day that sent him to the cross. Knowing that, Christians have always believed that in this world, even when we are at home, we cannot be entirely at ease. We know that here we have no continuing city, but we seek the city that is to come. Though it is right to love our home and our land, we dare not suppose that we are really yet "at home."

For when *we* say, "we would be in Jerusalem," we mean something more than that Israelite meant when he longed to be in Zion. When we sing the Lord's song we know that in human history we do it always as foreigners and exiles in a strange land. That Jerusalem for which we long and toward which we move is a kingdom that will stretch not just from shore to shore but from pole to pole, that will include peoples of every tongue — a kingdom in which the crucified One, risen and victorious, will alone reign.

For now then, on our pilgrim way, we can do no better than pray in the words the church gives us: Heavenly Father, you willed to make us citizens of your country and singers of your mercy. Do not abandon us in the land of exile, but bring us to the heavenly Jerusalem, chanting your praises; through Jesus Christ our Lord. Amen.

20. A Little Sleep

A little sleep, a little slumber,
*   a little folding of the hands to rest,*
and poverty will come upon you like a robber,
*   and want like an armed man.*

PROVERBS 24:33-34

And a great storm of wind arose, and the waves beat into
the boat, so that the boat was already filling. But Jesus
was in the stern, asleep on the cushion.

MARK 4:37-38

Though there are stranger books in the Bible, there are few more puzzling than Ecclesiastes. The author calls himself in Hebrew *Koheleth*, which is commonly translated "the Preacher." He is not very much like preachers we have known, however, and perhaps it is better if we simply call him Koheleth. Picture him now for yourselves. He is an old man and a deep thinker. Life has, in a sense, been good to him. He is not poverty-stricken; he has independence and leisure in his old age. He possesses marvelous talents and a gift for writing, so that we can be confident he must have been a successful and revered teacher of young Israelite boys. He has known the energy and heady enthusiasm of youth, the striving and achievement of middle age. He knows now the loneliness of old age. He has sought wisdom and justice, but learned to face the inevitable reality of injustice and the limits of human knowledge.

One scholar, Robert Gordis, pictures Koheleth when, as an old man, his former students return to visit him. Some of these students would have gone on to positions of importance in their world — whether as government officials, religious functionaries, or men of commerce. As he speaks with them, Koheleth

> notes that they have paid a high price for success. The shining, carefree countenances of youth, the sparkling eyes brimful with mischief, are gone. In their stead are worn faces, some drawn, others grown puffy with the years; and tired, unhappy eyes sagging beneath the weight of responsibility. . . . He knows what they have forgotten, that men's schemes and projects, their petty jealousies and labors, their struggles and heartaches, all are vanity and that joy in life is the one divine commandment.

And so he writes, "Go, eat your bread with enjoyment, and drink your wine with a merry heart; for God has already approved what you do. Let your garments always be white; let not oil be lacking on your head. Enjoy life with the wife whom you love, all the days of your vain life which he has given you under the sun, because that is your portion in life."

We strive all our life, writes Koheleth, and for what? To leave the fruits of our toil to others. They may be wise, but they may also be foolish and squander all for which we have toiled. They may enjoy without labor or responsibility the fruits of our days — and, significantly, nights — of labor. Koheleth knows surely the law of life in the passage from Proverbs that we heard at the outset.

> A little sleep, a little slumber,
>   a little folding of the hands to rest,
> and poverty will come upon you. . . .

That is the law of striving, and Koheleth knows it and knows that, in one sense, it is true. But he knows more. He has seen through that law of striving. Seen through it in his own life and those of his students we have pictured returning to visit him. He has seen the toll exacted by this law of striving, the price of pain and anxiety. So he says, "What has a man from all the toil and strain with which he toils beneath the sun? For all his days are full of pain, and his work is a vexation; even in the night his mind does not rest."

Koheleth has seen the effects of the law of striving in his own life and the lives of others. He has seen people struggle to succeed. He himself has sought wisdom and tried to plumb the hidden depths of God and God's creation. And for his pains he has had only sleepless nights without rest. His striving has been vanity — a striving after wind, something too insubstantial and fleeting ever to get a grip on. In the enthusiasm of youth and the achievement of middle age he sought justice and its fruits. Now he knows that the oppressors have power and the oppressed have only their tears. He has seen men pile up wealth and has learned that they are never satisfied. "He who loves money will not be satisfied with money," he tells us.

What is Koheleth's remedy for all this? Give up the law of striving, he says. Receive life as a gift from the hand of God and delight in it. There may be much that cannot be known and much that is evil, but life itself is to be prized. Koheleth does not say that we should give up toil; he says we should learn to give up striving. We should learn to receive rather than achieve. "There is nothing better for a man than that he should eat and drink, and find enjoyment in his toil. This also, I saw, is from the hand of God; for apart from him who can eat or who can have enjoyment? For to the man who pleases him God gives wisdom and knowledge and joy." That is Koheleth's insight: The joy of life comes only from God, and no amount of striving on our part can get it unless God gives it.

But who is capable of such things? Which of us can allow our life to be shaped by such receptivity? Where shall we find such a person among us? That is the great unanswered question in Ecclesiastes. Perhaps, though, we can suggest a criterion for identifying such a person: He must be one who knows how to sleep. Of him it must not be said, "even in the night his mind does not rest." Koheleth recommends the attitude expressed in Psalm 4:

> In peace I will both lie down and sleep;
> for thou alone, O LORD, makest me dwell in safety.

It is not easy just to lie down and sleep. Years ago I read John Barth's novel, *The End of the Road,* and I remember almost nothing of the story. But I do remember one of the characters saying that for him every night was a little suicide. I wonder if the same was not true for Koheleth; for though he is certainly right that life itself is a good in which we are to delight, it will be hard to sleep unless we know an even greater good.

Think of what we say about little children when they insist on calling us back time after time when they are in bed. The pretexts are many — drinks of water, trips to the bathroom, one more song, one more question, runny noses and scratchy throats, stuffed animals that fall out of bed, covers that won't stay put. Those are the pretexts. But what we say is that they just won't let themselves go and fall asleep. They're fighting it, we say, remembering perhaps from our youth truths about ourselves which we have long since repressed. We hear behind their excuses the truth about how hard it can be just to let go.

It is hard to do what the psalmist recommends: to lie down and sleep. That is, after all, something far different from falling into bed so bone-tired and utterly weary that we can no longer keep a grip on waking life. No, to lie down and sleep is deliberately to give over all the life that is ours into the keeping of God, entrusting ourselves utterly to his care. Where among us shall we find one who can do that? Not one who works or plays as long as he can until finally he falls exhausted into bed, but one who deliberately stops before he is that weary to have time for his prayers, time to say, "Now I lay me down to sleep; I pray thee, Lord, my soul to keep." Where shall we find a person who knows how to sleep?

I do not think Koheleth is our man. He says many times

that life is a delight, but it is the light of day that he loves. We catch from him no hint of beauty in the darkness and quiet of sleep. "Light is sweet," he writes, "and it is pleasant for the eyes to behold the sun. For if a man lives many years, let him rejoice in them all; but let him remember that the days of darkness will be many." Where shall we find one who knows how to sleep? The question becomes still more pressing when we remember that death is sometimes thought of as a sleep. Put in this still deeper perspective we may doubt even more whether Koheleth is our man. For the question now becomes not, "does he know how to sleep?" but, "does he know how to die?" Which means, does he know any higher good than life, anything or anyone that can so shape his life as to give him hope in death? "A living dog," says Koheleth, "is better than a dead lion" — almost like the little child screaming to play longer as we drag him off to bed.

Where shall we find among us one who knows how to sleep — and how to die? We have, of course, had that one before us from the very outset, but, nonetheless, it is important to name him. And so I point you again to the other passage I read when we began. "And a great storm of wind arose, and the waves beat into the boat, so that the boat was already filling. But Jesus was in the stern, asleep on the cushion."

There he is. One who can sleep. One who can truly say to his Father,

In peace I will both lie down and sleep;
     for thou alone, O LORD, makest me dwell in safety.

One also who knew how to die. Not pretending that it was an occasion for rejoicing, but willing even in Gethsemane and on the cross to see his Father's will through to the end, trusting that it was a gracious will. In him we are made new and set free — free to let his love take shape in our life, free to give up the law of striving until that day when God makes an end of it. Free, in other words, to sleep — to let go and, with security, give ourselves into God's keeping.

21. The End of the Day

And there came a man named Jairus, who was a ruler of the synagogue; and falling at Jesus' feet he besought him to come to his house, for he had an only daughter, about twelve years of age, and she was dying. . . . While he was still speaking, a man from the ruler's house came and said, "Your daughter is dead; do not trouble the Teacher any more." But Jesus on hearing this answered him, "Do not fear; only believe, and she shall be well." And when he came to the house, he permitted no one to enter with him, except Peter and John and James, and the father and mother of the child. And all were weeping and bewailing her; but he said, "Do not weep; for she is not dead but sleeping." And they laughed at him, knowing that she was dead. But taking her by the hand he called, saying, "Child, arise." And her spirit returned, and she got up at once.

LUKE 8:41-42, 49-55

"In the midst of life we are in death," the Scriptures say. Death surrounds us at every moment — and, indeed, is within us at every moment. The blood vessel in the brain that is one day going to rupture. The tumor that grows secretly and unseen. We live toward death while engaged in the simplest tasks of life and in every moment of life.

Helen went out last Tuesday to get some peaches, not knowing that she was going toward her death. I was called to the hospital around 4:00 in the afternoon, while I was loading the car to take one of my daughters off the next day for her first year of college. Which I did. And for two days I helped her get settled in that time of excitement and anticipation — at a moment in life when, on the one hand, possibilities seem endless, and when, on the other, we are learning a little more of what it means to say goodbye.

Knowing that I was returning for this funeral, I could not help reflecting that all of life — and of the way love takes shape in our lives with particular people to whom we are especially joined — all of life is preparing to say goodbye. In the midst of life we are in death. We never know for certain when our goodbye will be final.

When death comes, whether suddenly as it did for Helen or gradually, we experience it as an intruder — and as a mystery we cannot fully comprehend. Even though we have been living toward it every moment . . . even so, we can think of nothing to say. For we don't really know what death is — not from the inside. We cannot know it that way, and we are therefore speechless in the face of an event beyond our experience. We know death only as outsiders know it — never, until it is too late, from within.

But in the lesson we read from Luke's Gospel — the story

of Jairus' daughter — we get a hint of the difference between the outsider's and the insider's perspective on death. Jesus comes to the home of Jairus, and he says: "This child is not dead, but sleeping." The other people gathered there to mourn, who think they understand something about death, laugh at him, "knowing," as Luke writes, "that she was dead." But this man Jesus who says, "she is not dead, but sleeping," is One who knows death from the inside. He is Lord of life and death. He can take hold of death's mystery — and see through it. He knows, from the inside, that, powerful and dreadful as death is, there is One still stronger. So he can say, "this child is not dead, but sleeping."

You and I could not really say that on our own. We can only look at death from the outside and see it as a mystery. We can only shrink back a little from it in dread. And, of course, Jesus, one of us, knows death that way as well. He knows our life from the inside, so he knows that feeling of dread — as he knew it in Gethsemane. But he is also himself that One whom death cannot hold, for whom no goodbye need be final.

Helen Smith worshiped in this congregation Sunday after Sunday for much of her life. This was her congregation. When the service ended here last Sunday, we didn't know that we would be here today for her funeral. We didn't know that she would not worship here this coming Sunday. Last Sunday, her last Sunday here, the closing hymn was "Lord of All Hopefulness" — and it will be the closing hymn for us today. It gives us the words we cannot find on our own.

The hymn asks the Lord who has shared our life and shared even the death toward which our life inexorably moves, who has taken the measure of that death from the inside, to be with us in every moment.

- In our waking — at the break of day.
- In our working — at the noon of day.
- In our coming home — at the eve of day.
- In our sleeping — at the end of day.

"Be there at our sleeping, and give us, we pray, your peace in our hearts, Lord, at the end of the day" — and at the end of all our days.

This is a Lord who has taken the measure of death from the inside — and who lives. This is a Lord who can say of us, with that powerful creative word which he alone can speak, who can say of us as he has said of Helen: "This child is not dead, but sleeping."

In the midst of life we are in death. May we learn to number our days and to trust in every moment the presence of that Lord whose voice is contentment, and whose presence is balm.

V. Love as a Tangent toward Eternity in Time

"Who," the psalmist asks, "shall ascend the hill of the LORD?" And answers: "He who has clean hands and a pure heart." If love takes shape in our lives, and when it has fully taken shape in us, the blessing Jesus sets upon his followers will come true: "Blessed are the pure in heart; for they shall see God."

Because we are embodied souls, our love necessarily takes shape in time. Because we are ensouled bodies, our love seeks, finally, to rest in God. When we do so rest, our whole task, St. Augustine says, will be to praise God; for then, he says, nothing will remain but praise. Beginning from an attitude toward time rather different from Augustine's, Robert Jenson can close his two-volume systematic theology with a similar sentiment: "The end is music." And C. S. Lewis writes that "Joy is the serious business of heaven."

No doubt it would be possible to preach too much about heaven, but that is not likely to be our problem today. Unless we remember that all our loves must finally be directed to God, we are unlikely to love — here and now — as we ought.

We will ask of our finite loves more than they are meant to give — and in the process destroy them, if they do not first destroy us. The three sermons that follow, each rather different from the others, attempt to picture our life as a tangent toward eternity in time.

"Loving the Neighbor in God" was first published, under the title "Journey to Singing Mountain," in *Christianity Today* (April 25, 1975). Its inspiration was, I am sure, the following sentences from C. S. Lewis's *The Four Loves:* "It is probably impossible to love any human being simply 'too much.' We may love him too much *in proportion* to our love for God; but it is the smallness of our love for God, not the greatness of our love for the man, that constitutes the inordinacy." "Return with Us Now to Those Thrilling Days of Yesteryear" reflects, I have to admit, my childhood preoccupations. Nonetheless, I was pleased to find myself, as recently as April, 2001, able to see a Lone Ranger rerun on TV at 6:30 one morning. The approach to Stoicism in "Even the Sparrow Finds a Home," a sermon for All Saints' Day, is one I first learned many years ago from William Gass, in a graduate course in philosophy at Washington University (St. Louis). I confess to doubting whether he would find my use of it congenial, but a debt is a debt. The idea of "love as a tangent toward eternity in time" is borrowed loosely from a similar phrase in volume 2 of Reinhold Niebuhr's *The Nature and Destiny of Man.*

22. Loving the Neighbor in God

The autumn air was crisp and cool. The moon shone brightly and the stars twinkled merrily. Far off in the distance the Castle of the Great King on Singing Mountain was clearly evident in the moonlight. As the young man and woman walked slowly among the trees, the newly fallen leaves swirled playfully at their feet. "Good night, Alice," said the young man. "I must hurry or I will be late arriving home, and my father will again be displeased." He kissed her gently on the cheek. "Tomorrow night at the same time." With that he turned and ran quickly toward the lights of a cottage twinkling in the distance through the trees.

As Charles neared the cottage he was surprised to see it brightly lighted. "Father must have started fires in both fireplaces," Charles thought, but this was something done only on the coldest days of winter. Suddenly he realized that his father was standing at the door waiting for him. "Charles," said his father gravely, "there is a visitor to see you." He had never seen his father look quite this way. "The Great King himself from the Castle on Singing Mountain has come to see you. I do not know exactly why. Remember to act as is fitting to his dignity." The best Charles could manage was a feeble nod of the head. With that his father turned and led him into the brightly lighted room.

Entering the room Charles saw three men, dressed in the clothes of travelers. They looked much alike; yet somehow he had no doubt that the one seated nearest the fire was the Great King. He took several steps toward him until he remembered. "My Lord," he said, and bowed a bit clumsily. "I am Charles, thy faithful servant." To his surprise, the king rose from his chair and walked to where Charles was still attempting to bow.

"Rise, my son, and sit here by me near the fire, for I have come to talk with thee." Later Charles could remember little that the Great King had said to him. He remembered only that it had been a rather frightening experience, sitting that close to the Great King. Not that the king had been unkind. He was, to be sure, a stern and dignified man. Yet there was always a slight twinkle in his eyes — not the sort to make one take liberties or speak out of turn, but the sort that hints at untapped resources of good will.

One thing from that conversation Charles did remember for as long as he lived. "Charles, my son, I have come to call thee to the castle. No, thou canst not travel with me; for I have other tasks to fulfill before I return to the Castle on Singing Mountain. The task of journeying is thine, and the trip must be thine alone. But be assured, I shall be there when thy journey ends." Charles did not understand. He glanced quickly at his father, but his father's gaze was fixed firmly on the Great King. Charles had felt his heart leap at the words of the king. For what could be better than to travel to the castle? But still, he could not understand why the king had come to him and called him to make this journey. Then he remembered that it was not his place to keep the king waiting.

"If that is thy wish, my Lord, then I shall travel to thy castle."

"Good. Thou must leave at once. Thy father has packed food for thee. The moon will light thy way by night. Travel quickly, for the journey is not a short one."

"Tonight, my Lord?" Suddenly Charles' joy had vanished. What of Alice? Surely he could not leave without telling her why and bidding her farewell.

"Thou wishest to say goodbye to the fair maiden Alice, dost thou not?" Charles was so startled to find that the king knew his thoughts that he forgot all about using language appropriate to the dignity of the Great King. "Yes sir," he said, as if he were talking to the grocer — and blushed at the same time.

"Nevertheless, thou must leave tonight. But be of good cheer. For as surely as I am the Great King, thou hast my promise that the maiden Alice shall be thine." Then the king rose and turned to address Charles' father. "Well, good sir, canst thou provide lodging this night for me and my men? It appears that thou wilt have at least one extra room." With that he glanced at Charles, his eyes twinkling merrily.

"My Lord," said Charles' father, "to have thee lodge with us is both our bounden duty and our delight."

"Excellent," replied the Great King. "But first thou must say farewell to young Charles and bid him Godspeed on his journey."

That was all Charles could remember. The firm handshake of his father as he wished him quick and safe travel.

The gentle and tearful embrace of his mother. It had been four days since Charles had set out from the cottage, and soon he would be entering the foothills of Singing Mountain. The nearer he came, the more his joy increased. The trees, the wind, the lakes, the leaves — all appeared to join in a song that seemed to Charles to be coming from the Castle of the Great King. Yet there was always a touch of sadness in his joy. What must Alice be thinking of him? Would she imagine that he had forgotten the promises he had made to her?

And, to tell the truth, Alice did not quite understand. She had waited for Charles the next evening. Again the following evening she had waited. Finally, on the fourth day of his absence, plucking up her courage, she had spoken to Charles' father as he worked in the fields. It had been a brief conversation, but his father had been surprisingly gentle and kind — as if he understood her grief only too well. He told her, as simply as he could, the story of the visit of the Great King.

"But why could not Charles have come to bid me farewell, even as he did to you and his mother? Is his love for the king so great that it destroys his love for me?" Charles' father was silent, and Alice blurted out: "No doubt the king warned him not to love me too much."

"Alice," said Charles' father, "you are young, and you must learn to speak with greater care. Yet I understand what you say. Do you not think that his mother and I are sad to see him leave so hurriedly?"

"But then the same is true in your case," Alice said, feeling more insistent all the time. "For it seems that in order to love the Great King, Charles must love you and me and his mother less. If that is true, I do not know why we should love the Great King at all."

"Careful, Alice." Charles' father had himself thought many of the things that Alice now put into words. "These are deep questions that you ask, and I do not know the answers. I can only tell you what I think, for the king has not explained these matters to me. To love you without loving the Great King would be to love you not like a maiden but, rather, like a king. I do not think it is possible for Charles to love you too much, nor do I think the Great King wants him to love you less than he does. No, Alice, that cannot be. It is not possible for Charles to love you too much. It is only possible for him to love the king too little. That is what I think."

"And yet," said Alice, a bit more slowly and thoughtfully, "the king does not really need Charles. And I do need him — very much." Blushing, she glanced quickly to the ground.

"True," said Charles' father, "the Great King does not need him. But Charles needs the king." Then he bent over and picked up his tools. "And now, Alice, I must get back to my work, for the sun will soon be setting."

As the sun finished its journey to western lands on that fourth day, Charles entered the foothills of the mountain. Suddenly he realized that two men were traveling with him. No one said a word for a long time; all attention was fixed on the Castle of the Great King, which now seemed much nearer.

"Stupidity!" The word startled Charles out of his reverie. It had been spoken by the stranger on his left, the man whom Charles ever after called simply "the terrible stranger." Here in the foothills of the mountain, where everything seemed alive with song, it sounded to Charles worse by far than any curse word he had ever heard.

"Stupidity!" repeated the terrible stranger. "And to think

that fools actually imagine the singing comes from the castle."

"And dost thou not, my friend?" asked the other traveler, the one whom Charles called simply "the kind stranger."

"Of course not," replied the other, "for I know where it comes from. I have been there — to the cave of many delights by a lake near here. There one can find dancing and singing and reveling all night long. That is where the song comes from. There by the lake the ground is lush and fertile. Why would anyone want to go up the mountain to that castle where all is cold and barren?"

"Mayhap that shall prove true. But methinks the song in the cave may prove to be but an echo of music from the castle and the reveling but figures of shadows on the wall of the cave."

The terrible stranger looked as if he would curse, but just then Charles spoke for the first time. "Excuse me, sir," he said, addressing the kind stranger, "but why do you speak in that manner when the Great King is not here?"

"We are in the foothills of Singing Mountain, my son," he replied. "And I never speak any other way here. It is a sign of respect for the Great King."

"He has called me to his castle, you know," Charles said. "He visited me at my father's cottage and told me to come to him at his castle." And then, as the words rushed out, Charles told the strangers about the visit of the king, about his joy, and about his love for Alice and his sorrow at leaving her.

"It doth not surprise me," said the kind stranger.

"Well," broke in the terrible stranger, "I don't understand anything about late-night visits of the Great King or about song coming from this castle, but I do understand the sorrow of the boy at leaving a beautiful young damsel. In fact, I too have left my wife for the sake of my calling. It was a tearful farewell, but I was firm. One must be strong and pitiless if one hopes to achieve noble deeds."

"Ah, but dost thou truly think the cases similar?" interjected the other stranger. "For the Great King hath not asked young Charles to give up his love for fair Alice. In fact, it seemeth that he hath expressly promised that the maiden shall be his. No, methinks the cases are quite unlike."

"But noble sir," broke in Charles, beginning like the kind stranger to talk as if the Great King were present, "dost thou truly think the Great King wishest me to love fair Alice? For it seemeth that I dare not love her too much if I am to love him as he hath commanded."

"My son, I tell thee truly, thou canst not love Alice too much. Thou canst only love the Great King too little."

At this the terrible stranger could restrain himself no longer. "Fools' talk! Fools' talk! The only thing to be loved is life at the cave of many delights. There life is good — not cold and stark as on the mountain."

"Perhaps," said the kind stranger, "but it is not to the cave that young Charles hath been called. The Great King is not to be found there. And I should think that the most lovely place in the world would be void and bare were not the Great King there with me."

"Come, come," said the terrible stranger, with a very funny (but also a little frightening) look on his face. "Let us not argue. It is dark. Shall we not make camp together tonight? Let us sit by the fire, and I shall tell you some stories about the cave of many delights." Even as he spoke he was guiding Charles off the path into a small clearing among the trees. Charles had not really intended to stop. He was eager to push on and finish his journey to the castle. But the stranger's hand was strong and firm, and Charles felt he had almost no choice. He was glad to see that the kind stranger had joined them.

For several hours at least they sat by the fire and — true to his word — the terrible stranger told story after story of the happy life to be found at the cave. And always as he talked he looked directly at Charles. Finally, weary from the long journey, Charles lay down beneath an ancient oak tree and was quickly fast asleep.

How long he slept he never knew. He woke suddenly in the darkness to hear the kind stranger saying to him, "Quickly now, my son. Quickly. Do not stop until thou hast reached the castle. It will not be far."

"Why? Will you come along, good sir?" asked Charles. Yet even as he spoke, he knew it could not be.

"No, my son. The Great King hath not called me to the castle just yet. I must stay here to deal with our traveling companion." At that Charles thought he heard someone coming toward them. "Now, off with thee. And do not stop, no matter what thou hearest. Farewell, my son, and God speed thee to the castle."

Charles was on his feet and running before he realized what was happening. He thought he heard behind him the sound of men struggling, but, finding the path, he ran straight toward the castle. As he approached the gate of the castle, Charles saw the sentry standing guard. He tried to decide how to explain that he had been called to the castle by the Great King, but before he could decide the gate swung open.

Charles entered the courtyard, breathless from his run. Immediately he saw another member of the palace guard, who said to him, "This way, sir. They await thee in the great banquet hall."

He led Charles to a magnificent oak door and swung it open. The room was flooded with light, and for a moment Charles was dazzled by it. Inside the banquet room were countless guests, all dressed in beautiful garments. As Charles entered, a man — who he later learned was a steward — stepped up and put on him too a beautiful garment. At that moment the Great King saw Charles, and he came across the banquet hall, walking quickly, yet in a stately manner. All eyes turned to gaze at Charles as he bowed before the king.

"Rise, my son. Thou hast come even as I asked of thee. Welcome to the banquet hall of the Castle on Singing Mountain. Dost thou know why thou art here? We have called thee here so that we may celebrate with thee. For in this castle there must always be singing. And what better occasion for merriment shall we find than thy marriage to lovely Alice?"

Charles did not know why he had not seen her sooner. Perhaps it was because his attention had been focused on the Great King. But it was true. There beside the king stood Alice, looking lovelier than ever before. "I have promised her to thee, my son," said the Great King, "and she shall be thine."

"And now," he said in a voice that was suddenly very loud and very regal, "now, my guests, let there be singing and merriment."

And solemnly but joyously Charles said to no one in particular, "And may the Great King be praised forever."

23. Return with Us Now to Those Thrilling Days of Yesteryear

For now we see in a mirror dimly, but then face to face.

I CORINTHIANS 13:12

Those my age grew up in the days when television was just beginning to make its impact on American homes. Many of us can remember our families getting their first television sets when we were young. The fare was varied. We used to rush home from school to watch Howdy Doody. A few years later the Mouseketeers and Spin & Marty captured the attention of scores of us. But most of all, I myself remember the westerns: Cisco Kid, Roy Rogers, Wild Bill Hickok, Hopalong Cassidy, Annie Oakley, and many more.

Our parents were worried at the time lest we watch too many westerns. I have not forgotten the anxiety of having to choose between Roy Rogers and Cisco Kid. In retrospect, however, it seems pretty clear to me that the themes of the westerns are perennial. What is Star Wars, after all, except a good old-fashioned, shoot-em-up western, set this time in outer space?

Inadequacies from the artistic point of view there may have been in those westerns, but they touched themes near the center of all our lives: The constant struggle of good against evil. The sense that commitment to the good may be risky, that it may have to be an act of faith. The clear perception that anyone unwilling to risk such commitment must finally be swallowed up by the forces of evil. Ready illustrations of the importance of faithfulness in human life.

But in addition to all those themes, one of the old westerns was also about identity. I watched it faithfully as a child; I have watched its reruns many times as an adult. The story of the Lone Ranger is a story about a hidden, mysterious identity — about a man who comes masked, not out of a desire to puzzle or terrify, but simply because that is the only way he can carry out his mission. (Of course, in order to understand that one must have seen the very first episode, which tells how the Lone Ranger came to be in the first place.) Return with me now to those thrilling days of yesteryear — and ponder the mystery of the Lone Ranger.

Think first of his *work*. How would we describe what he does? We would not be wrong to latch onto language that has a biblical ring. He casts down the mighty who have exalted themselves. The episodes of the Lone Ranger surely never provided any comfort to the respectable and established. There are crooked sheriffs, and respected citizens turn out to be the enemies of their neighbors and townspeople.

The Lone Ranger does more than cast down the proud, however; he binds up the wounded and brings healing and reconciliation where there is bitterness and strife. How many episodes did we not watch in which conflict between the cattlemen and the settlers establishing their homesteads threatened to erupt into a bloody range war? And how often was there not behind such conflict some scheming, ruthless (indeed, if you will, devilish) individual seeking to profit by others' losses? And how often was not such conflict narrowly averted by decisive and reconciling action on the part of the Lone Ranger?

The healing which the Lone Ranger brings is no sentimental sweetness, despite the artistic inadequacies which may sometimes make it seem that way. For there is no suggestion that this reconciliation can come easily. No suggestion that it can come until those evil, scheming men have been overcome. There is a real clash between good and evil which must end not in compromise but in defeat for one and victory for the other.

That is true of the Lone Ranger's work. What of his *person*? Remember how in Mark's Gospel, when Peter identifies Jesus as the Christ — that is, as Messiah — Jesus warns the disciples to say nothing of this. And he goes on to speak of himself in other terms. We might also recall the occasion when — also in Mark's Gospel — Pilate asks Jesus whether he is king of the Jews. To which Jesus replies, with seemingly studied ambiguity, "You have said so." And scholars of the New Testament have puzzled over the seeming reluctance on Jesus' part to acknowledge his true identity.

Now, we should not play down the scholarly problem; for it is a genuine one. But for those reared on the Lone Ranger the difficulties may seem less intense. How often did we not see episodes in which the Lone Ranger shows to a doubting sheriff a silver bullet, and the sheriff asks: "So, then, you're the Lone Ranger?"

Watch as many reruns as you like, and never once I think

will you hear the Lone Ranger answer in the affirmative. Most often he simply smiles and says, "All right, then, here's the plan I have in mind. . . ." And never once does the youthful (or, even, somewhat older) viewer feel that anything important has been left unsaid. When the signs are present, direct statement is unnecessary, even crass. And so, we can paraphrase Jesus' words to the disciples of John the Baptist: "Go and tell the sheriff what you have seen: a masked man with an Indian companion, the masked man's great white horse, his silver bullets." Is that not an answer to any doubting query? Could any more convincing reply be given?

And yet, of course, some do still doubt, don't they? Can we, after all, really trust a masked man? Is that not the sign of an outlaw, of one who seeks to hide his identity? How are we to be certain that in this one case there are (as the Lone Ranger always says) "good reasons" for hiding his identity? How are we to know that the mask is the sign of one who fights for justice and right rather than one who comes to rob and spoil? Or, what is still worse, if we commit ourselves to him, if we put his (perhaps daring) plan into action, and he turns out to be a fraud — what then? Something worse than robbery or even death will then be our lot. We shall be ridiculed and scorned. It is perhaps natural, therefore, that some still doubt. To one who sees, the signs are no longer ambiguous. But the signs provide no absolute proof, no assurance that cannot be questioned.

So, then, we must put the question directly and bluntly: "Well, masked man, it sounds good, but how do I know you're telling me the truth? Why should I believe you?" And those of us who have watched long enough and often enough to know the reply could answer for that masked man without a moment's hesitation. "You'll just have to trust me, sheriff." At that moment the choice is made, though it seems (at least to the viewer) that the sheriff is not so much choosing as simply making the only possible response to the Lone Ranger's call for commitment.

And come what may, the commitment that stems from that encounter has sustaining power. The plans may seem to go awry. It may even seem on occasion that the Lone Ranger has badly misjudged the situation. But the memory of that first meeting leads a man on, makes him willing to risk defeat rather than betray that trust. Surely Tonto himself is the archetype of the committed follower. If Tonto seems more certain of the Lone Ranger than many others, more devoted to his plans, that is surely because Tonto has been with him longer. He has on more than one occasion been rescued from danger by the daring of the Lone Ranger. And their years of association have served only to strengthen the commitment made at their first meeting. The basic answer, whether the question is posed by Tonto, a sheriff, or a confused rancher, is always the same: "You'll just have to trust me."

But finally, is it too much to say that the true Lone Ranger fan cannot miss the end-time expectation that permeates the entire story? One who had watched only a few episodes, a dilettante, might well misunderstand that expectation. He might think that the end-time would come when the West was safely settled, robbers and rustlers rooted out, and peace and joy established. And no doubt that is part of the end-time expectation. Surely, however, there is more, and one who has been not just an occasional onlooker but a genuine follower of the Lone Ranger cannot for a moment doubt that there is more.

What is it for which the devoted viewer waits? Without hesitation I answer: For the day when the Lone Ranger will take off his mask and permit me to see him face to face.

Many have tried to unmask him, but that cannot be. He himself will take that action when his mission has been accomplished. Surely, on that day the West will be settled, and peace and joy will reign. But all that is incidental. For what is truly important to the committed follower is that on that day we shall see him as he is. The mask will be gone forever. And there will be no need for reruns.

24. Even the Sparrow Finds a Home

The Prayer of the Day for All Saints' Day says concisely but precisely what the day is about: Almighty God, whose people are knit together in one holy church, the body of Christ our Lord, grant us grace to follow your saints of old in lives of faith and commitment, and to know the inexpressible joys you have prepared for those who love you.

The emphasis here is on the whole church; for this is a feast of that whole church: the church militant (those still in this life) and the church triumphant (the faithful warriors who have triumphed in the fight and now enjoy their sabbath rest). Our prayer is that the faith of those triumphant saints may sustain us in our pilgrimage. We are to see that what counts about them is the One in whom they believed. And we are not to stifle within ourselves the longing for a joy greater than is ever given in this life, what the prayer terms the inexpressible joys prepared for those who love God.

But how shall we speak of such things today, in a world that often seems to have stifled its longing for God? We can tell a story — a story told first by Seneca, one of the great

Stoic philosophers of Rome. Stoicism is a philosophical school usually said to have begun with the philosopher Zeno in the fourth century B.C. and to have continued through the great Emperor Marcus Aurelius into the second century A.D. It no longer exists as an identifiable school of thought, but it continues to be influential and is always, in certain ways, the chief alternative to Christian faith.

Seneca tells a story about a man named Stilbo, who, according to Seneca, displayed the ideal Stoic spirit. Stilbo's country was captured and his wife and children killed by a conqueror named Demetrius, who was also called Sacker of Cities because of the general devastation he brought upon those he conquered. As Stilbo emerges from the desolation, his wife and children dead, alone and yet happy, Demetrius mockingly asks him whether he has lost anything. To which Stilbo replies: "I have all my goods with me." And Seneca says of this: "There is a brave and stout-hearted man for you! The enemy conquered, but Stilbo conquered his conqueror. 'I have lost nothing!' . . . 'My goods are all with me!' In other words, he deemed nothing that might be taken from him to be a good."

That one little story gives the essence of the Stoic spirit better than countless lectures could. The Stoic strives for self-sufficiency. And if he succeeds in achieving it, no one can hurt him. He could lose nothing that would really matter. Stilbo emerges from the general devastation having lost everything, as we might say. But he says: All my goods are with me. I have lost nothing.

When I read a Stoic like Seneca with students, I usually say: Stoicism is, in some respects, a very practical doctrine. It will work. Do what the Stoics tell you, practice detachment, do not rest your heart in any thing or person — and no one will ever be able to hurt you. No one can tear you to pieces by taking away someone you love. Stoicism will work. The only question is, Do you want what it offers?

This may seem a long-winded way into a sermon, but it identifies for us a crucial question. Do we want what such a view offers? Or does it miss some central features of human existence? For us who understand ourselves in terms of the Bible's story of creation and redemption, a Stoic attitude could never be satisfactory. It misses too much of the truth of life.

It misses, first, part of what it means to be the creatures we are. We are embodied. We are not just souls attached to no particular time and place. We are tied by our Creator to a here-and-now, put here by that Creator and bound to each other. He sets the solitary in families. He gives us friends and loved ones, fellow believers. And he teaches us that as we are dependent on him, so are we dependent on one another.

With us there can be no ideal of self-sufficiency, no struggle to be completely independent. Think of the symbolism of human birth. There is not one of us who did not spend nine months or thereabouts in our mother's womb, living not only in her but also off her. We should see there a striking parable of our dependence. To turn from those whom the Creator gives us is, in Christian terms, quite simply the first step on the road to hell. For what the Stoic wants, self-sufficiency and dependence on no one, the Christian calls hell. No one is more self-sufficient than Satan. God, by contrast, is not content to be a single, self-sufficient monad, but is a threefold union in love.

Of course, to commit ourselves to others is to take a great risk. We will not have them forever. As they have been given us, so will they be taken from us. Human life lived out in love means acceptance of that risk. It means a willingness to give ourselves in bonds of love which we cannot finally sustain. When the day comes that we lose the one we love, we will learn sorrow. And we ought to. That is part of what it means to be a human being.

We can be self-sufficient if we like. Stoicism may work. But in order to make it work we are going to have to kill within us something essential to our nature: the particular bonds of love and affection which the Creator gives us. That the Stoic misses.

Nor is that all. The Stoic misses also the longing buried deep within the human heart. Our hearts are restless, St. Augustine writes, until they rest in God. That restlessness, that longing for God, is captured beautifully by the psalmist.

> How lovely is thy dwelling place,
>   O LORD of hosts!
> My soul longs, yea, faints
>   for the courts of the LORD;
> my heart and flesh sing for joy
>   to the living God.
> Even the sparrow finds a home,
>   and the swallow a nest for herself,
>   where she may lay her young,
> at thy altars, O LORD of hosts. . . .
> Blessed are those who dwell in thy house
>   ever singing thy praise!

This is not, primarily, a desire to live a little longer or to live again, or even to be reunited with loved ones. It is, first and above all, a longing for God: the One for whom we are made, the One from whom we are estranged. And if throughout our lives, no matter how many or great our blessings, there remains some sense of restlessness, some longing still unsatisfied, that is the restless heart which cannot rest but in God. If we have the sense that, no matter how settled we may become we are never quite at home, that we have here no continuing city, well . . . that need not surprise those who long for a city whose light is the glory of God. Even the sparrow finds a home, the psalmist says, and we are entitled to hope that we shall too.

This hope the Stoic misses. There are, perhaps, only two ways to come to terms with the sorrow and incompletion of life. We can tell ourselves that it is finally of no account; we can practice Stoic resignation to our fate, whatever it may be. Or we may dare to hope that God will, one day, do better. The Stoic will not hope for more. For him, the Father of all is an indifferent father — indifferent, ultimately, to our fate. And we had better therefore resign ourselves to that fate.

But the Christian is a most immoderate person — trusting that our Father is not indifferent but is a loving Father. Trusting that he will be that for us because he was that for Jesus. That trust is what made the saints saints. Not anything they did, but the One in whom they believed. Seneca's ideal Stoic says, "I have all my goods with me." The saints whom we remember today say — and say eternally — "I have all my goods with thee."

The departed saints, like the sparrow, have found a home. We are still pilgrims, longing for the courts of the Lord. Yet, "all are one in thee, for all are thine." Quite rightly, therefore, we pray: Almighty God, whose people are knit together in one holy church, the body of Christ our Lord, grant us grace to follow your saints of old in lives of faith and commitment, and to know the inexpressible joys you have prepared for those who love you; through your Son, Jesus Christ our Lord. Amen.